# Stand out

# Fit in

# Have fun

Career progress for people who enjoy life

Eyesore Ltd. Cambridge

Published by Eyesore Ltd
Cambridge

Website: www.eyesore.ltd.uk/standout
Email: books@eyesore.ltd.uk
To order please visit the website or contact 'Eyesore Ltd' at
5 Phillips Street, Risca, Gwent NP11 6DF

First published in Great Britain in 2006
Copyright © Jane Phillips 2006

ISBN 10: 0-9554665-0-4
ISBN 13: 978-0-9554665-0-2

Cartoons and cover illustrations by Blake Pheasey

# Contents

## To begin

## chapter one
## Us

## chapter two
## Being likeable

## chapter three
## Our world

## chapter four
## Communicating

chapter eight
# Learning

chapter nine
# What next?

# And finally

# Acknowledgements

# Questions, Questions

# About the author

# To begin

## ... new century – new style

At the end of the 20th century, if you wanted to 'get on' in your career, you didn't spend precious time and effort 'getting on' with your fellow workers. Promotion meant competition – and that could include climbing over colleagues to get to the top. In the 21st century, the clever people have realised that competing isn't the answer. The work environment has changed and will keep on changing. In this unstable world, the ground is shifting and there is no safe and secure career path. On shifting ground the safest option is to tie yourself to others – so, getting on with people becomes an imperative. But that won't be enough to guarantee success. You'll also have to stand out from the crowd.

In a business world where stability is no longer an option, it is the nice, smart people who will survive and prosper. Why? Because they have the appropriate skills to deal effectively with a changing environment – and these skills favour co-operation over competition. In order to succeed, they will have to jump from job to job climbing steadily as they go. They will need the skills and knowledge to ensure that they are selected, retained and promoted – not once but many times. And when they get to the top, it is those self-same skills that will keep them there.

The surest way for you to get on in your career, and to stay on top, is to manage those two opposites; you must fit in and stand out – and do them simultaneously!

It sounds impossible but it's really not that difficult – if you follow these six basic principles:

Be likeable

Communicate with head and heart

Network for win/win

Self-market appropriately

Lead honestly

Learn continuously.

You can progress in your career – and with the right skills and knowledge you can do this without compromising your principles. Progress in the 21$^{st}$ century requires that you continuously upgrade your knowledge base, use your communicative style to gain influence and market yourself, network all the time and everywhere and effortlessly win friends and allies. And, to do all this successfully, you need to understand and foster your likeable traits – those parts of your personality which make you irresistibly attractive.

## Choices, choices!

This book might have been called

*Get on by getting on; How to climb the career ladder without treading on fingers*

or

*You don't have to be a pig to eat all the cake; Career progress for likeable people*

but eventually I plumped for a title that included the concept of fun. The reason? In our rush-and-hurry world it is easy to overlook those things that really make life worthwhile – to forget to enjoy life. So this is a gentle reminder that we only get one chance at life so let's go for it – and live!

We spend most of our waking hours and most of our adult life at work so that's a good place to start.

Why should you read on?

If you want to get on in your career, but also to enjoy your working life, this book provides the information you need. But it's your choice how much you swallow! Because this book is also about the choices we make and the future we create. If it causes you to question – then my task will be done!

*Stand out - Fit in - Have fun*

# chapter one

# Us

## ... where we come from

So, you've never thought of yourself as a time traveller? Don't worry, you haven't picked up a science fiction book by mistake. This is science fact. We're *all* time travellers. Just by living our lives, we are taking a journey across time. And what a time we've chosen!

We enter this world at a particular point in human history, we travel through time and then we leave it again. At life's arrival gate we were totally dependent on others and incontinent in mind and body. We'll probably reach the departure lounge in precisely the same state. But, that's some way ahead!

Throughout most of the intervening years, your life is your own and you can choose precisely how you are going to live it. You can change the direction of your life's journey at any time. You may decide that you're in the wrong job and make a complete change, mid-career. More fundamentally though, you can decide to change who you are. For most of us, the only thing that stops us from becoming what we really want to be is our belief that we cannot change. Once we have dispensed with the self-limiting factors that hold us back, it is amazing what we can accomplish.

This is fortunate because, at the beginning of the 21st century, our human capability to adapt to a changing world is being tested as never before. As long ago as 1964, Bob Dylan wrote, 'The times, they are a'changing'. In retrospect, we realise he should have followed up with, 'And boy, you ain't seen nothin' yet!' It's not environmental change (though that's a concern) but man-made change which will create the most problems and opportunities for those of us who live in the developed world. In evolutionary terms, the ultimate reality is that we adapt or perish, so the decision is not difficult. That isn't to say that the people who don't take advantage of these changes will die. They won't – but they will be the also-rans who form the underclass of the future.

## What are we like

In order to make the most of our ability to adapt, we need to understand ourselves better. The world is evolving and so are we. As members of this human race – what are we like? Whether we like it or not, evolution has taken us out of our caves but it hasn't quite taken cave mentality out of us. We are still subject to certain basic instincts which were the survival mechanisms of our cave ancestors.

First the bad news; human beings are irrational, selfish, self-deluding and dependent on others. On the face of it, this doesn't seem a good starting point for a book about nice, smart, successful people who enjoy life! But they are all just a normal part of being human. They are the survival mechanisms which have helped to ensure the continuity of the human race. If we are to continue to survive and prosper in our increasingly complex world, then understanding where we come from could prove crucial.

### Irrational

You think you are rational? Not so. We are controlled by hormones which, in turn, control our emotions. We have limited control over the emotions we experience – though we do retain almost total control over the actions we take as a result of those emotions. You don't need to be old or a follower of Star Trek to have heard of Mr Spock who was half human and half Vulcan – the latter race being truly rational. There were many things on his human side which he found 'did not compute'.

Here are just some of the irrational things we do:

It would be rational to support the football team most likely to win. But do we? Of course not! We have an emotional attachment to 'our' team which endures through good times and bad.

It would be rational to vote for a political party purely on the basis of its policies. Do we? No, we are swayed by the physical attractiveness or otherwise of the party leaders – and whether or not they have hair! Why else would politicians spend vast sums on image consultants and voice coaches? It's a pity about the hair though – neither shiny pates nor wigs seem to work.

It would be rational to decide that we cannot foretell the future. But perhaps the time and money spent on fortune-telling, be it through astrology, Tarot readings or crystal balls, is not wasted – if it makes people feel more secure in an uncertain world.

It would be rational, when we choose our friends, to look for equality for both sides of the relationship. But do we? We don't, and thank goodness for that. We let our hearts rule our heads but contemplating the opposite sends shivers down the spine. If we let our heads choose our friends, what a cold and calculating world that would be.

This emotional / rational dynamic – heart and head – is not confined to our private lives; it surfaces at work too.

All the decisions we take, all the choices we make are to some extent ruled by our emotions – they do not compute. And thank goodness for that; I, for one, don't want to be a Vulcan!

## Selfish

Do you believe that you are selfish? Well, if you do, you'd be right. We are pre-programmed to seek advantage for ourselves and our own. It is in our nature to 'look after number one'. As young children, we were entirely self-centred. We believed that the universe revolved around us. Most of us, but not all, have grown beyond this phase and have learned that other people have equal and sometimes superior rights. We have learned to value other people. We also perform actions which *appear* to be selfless. The qualification in that last sentence may seem cynical. But for almost all altruistic activities, we get a pay-back. Many people work as volunteers and their motivations for doing so are complex. But if they get no return on their investment, be it through a sense of achievement, a sense of community, increased feelings of self-worth or any of a myriad of rewards, they cease their volunteering activity. We only continue with activities which give us long or short term gain. We may not consciously search for 'what's in it for me' but if there is no benefit, be it financial or emotional, we eventually cease that activity.

## Self-deluding

Do you ever delude yourself? Yes, you do – all the time. And this is absolutely essential for your continued self-esteem. Our own personal view of ourselves is different from anyone else's. Others see us from their different perspectives and they very seldom tell us exactly what they think of us. This may well be a good thing but it means that we have to pick up subliminal messages. Information which fits our self-concept is easily assimilated. But our psyche is very adept at either filtering out those messages which will damage our self-esteem so that they never enter our consciousness, or of skewing their meaning to fit with our perception of ourselves. Our memory is so adept at this that we even remember compliments which were never uttered!

Not convinced? Then why do we cringe at photos of ourselves? People say, 'What a good likeness', when staring out at us is the image of our parent and not ourselves. Uggh! Why is it a shock when we catch a sudden glimpse of ourselves in a shop window and we look fatter, older, and with worse posture that our self image believes? In each case it is because our self-image dictates that we will remain misinformed.

Why do we rationalise our decision not to help someone in need by deciding he was drunk, on drugs and probably violent? Worse still, we may behave similarly towards disabled people. In an experiment, fewer people stopped to help a person in distress who was in a wheelchair than one who was able-bodied. When asked why, they shuffled with shame. They offered a myriad of excuses; they would normally have stopped but they were late for work, they were strangers in the town, they had an urgent appointment, etc, etc. Their action had not fitted their self-image of a Good Samaritan so there had to be a good reason!

Why don't any of us think we are dislikeable? Actually, some people do and this again relates to self-image. People with low self-esteem often dislike themselves and believe that others feel similarly towards them. Sadly, their self-delusory mechanisms have failed to protect them. For the rest of us, we are thoroughly surprised when we find that someone doesn't like us. How could they be so wrong!

## Dependent

Do you need other people? Yes, of course you do! The number of people we need will vary from person to person. Some of us will need to relate to a large group of friends and acquaintances, while others need fewer people. Our need for others is both rational and emotional. We know that the maintenance of society depends on a web of relationships and emotionally, we depend on others for both intimacy and friendship, which are both key to our psychological well-being. There are a few, and they are very few, people who do not enter into any relationships with others. In years gone by, they were treated with suspicion and superstition – but they had a purpose. Hermits were seen as a conduit to God or in possession of magical powers. Thus, they were accommodated as it was thought sensible to stay on their right side! Their purpose has disappeared but these people continue to be treated with both suspicion and superstition.

You might think that our innate selfishness would automatically work in opposition to our need to relate to others. If we're looking after number one, how can we be the nice, kind, loving people who form good relationships? Sometimes these two do work in opposition and we all know selfish people who trample over the sensitivities of others. However, these two human traits can and do work in synchrony to create win/win relationships. These relationships are beneficial to both parties and are based on both rational and emotional ties. The sound and long lasting relationships will also be based on truth – so self delusion must be addressed. And who succeeds best in creating and maintaining these positive relationships? People who are likeable of course!

## Basic instincts plus

And there is more good news. The description above has elements of truth but tells only half the story. It is the intangibles; the higher order human traits, the need for spiritual, moral and aesthetic outlets which makes the human race so awesome. They come as a by-product of being (possibly) the only species of animal capable of self-reflection.

Just think how beauty and truth can tug at our emotions. It might be a piece of music or poetry; it could be a sunset, a violent storm or a pattern of ice crystals which stirs your emotions. Compassion fatigue aside, which of us has remained unmoved by the reporting of some natural disaster – or worse still, a man-made one? The splendour of the natural world together with music, art, poetry and other man-made expressions of beauty, have the power to evoke strong feelings, as does our exposure to unpalatable truth. Of course, there is also a downside. Just as those artists in music, pictures and words can elicit constructive emotions, so it is easy, for those who know how, to drum up destructive emotions. We can just as easily be moved to hatred as to love. For all our complexity, as a race we humans can be extraordinarily naïve!

However, and whenever, we feel these keen emotions, it is in these that we find the basis of our humanity. They reflect the difference between us and other animals (and Vulcans!)

Before going on to think about how we might choose to change ourselves it is important to address briefly the issue of vulnerability. There are times in all our lives when we feel emotionally robust and can face whatever the world throws at us. At other times, we are much more vulnerable to emotional highs and lows. If you've recently been dealt a double or even a single whammy, you will need time for your emotions to recover. This might be a time for consolidation rather than change. Sensitivity to your own vulnerabilities and to those of others makes the building and maintaining of relationships a much more secure endeavour.

## The truth behind this book

A few years ago, on my life's journey, I stumbled on a disconcerting truth about myself. I realised that my treatment of those I liked was very different from my treatment of those I disliked. I was not being fair. Following up on this, I found that I was not alone – far from it. In every case I have come across in my research, the same distinction holds true. We all treat the people we like more favourably than those we don't. And it's the same at home, at work, in the pub, everywhere.

If we compare our treatment of people we like with those we dislike; for people we dislike:

• We give them less of our time and attention.

• We take less notice of what they say.

• We are less tolerant of their shortcomings and failures.

• We are less prepared to acknowledge their strengths.

• We give more weight to their weaknesses.

• We are less prepared to assist them.

• And we often go out of our way to avoid them.

In the world of the present and the world we are entering, this could have serious consequences for them.

## chapter two

# Being likeable

## ... how to get on with everyone (well, almost)!

The unexpected discovery that I was treating people I liked more favourably than those I didn't led me to ask myself some tough questions. What was it that made the difference between those people I liked, those I was indifferent to and those I actively disliked? That was the easy part! Relationships work both ways, so I also had to do some rather uncomfortable soul searching about my own 'likeability quotient'. I had gained some inkling about the traits I liked in others – but was I exhibiting those traits myself? And for someone who believes equal treatment to be important, there was also the vexing question of fair treatment for all. Enough of the introspection! I had to discover whether other people shared my views. I wanted to know if there are universal or even general 'likeability' traits. Is there a discernible pattern of factors which are likeable or, because relationships rely on our own characteristics as much as those of other people, is it just a random mess?

The good news is that it's not a random mess – therefore we can learn something from it. But it does take some time and effort to put that learning into effect – I know because I'm trying to do it. The effort lies not in changing behaviour, which is relatively easy, but in the deeper changes in attitudes and value system which are required. But there is more good news – it's worth it. I've put more effort into being interested and friendly with people, but above all, in truly valuing them. As a result, I'm happier, more alive, more perceptive and more in tune with people that I've ever been.

I asked other people. So, what did they tell me about likeability? In order to gather a variety of perspectives, I interviewed people who were of different personality types (using the Myers Briggs Type Indicator). They were of both sexes and a variety of ages. These people were also chosen because I knew them to be thoughtful and reflective. This was not a research project in the academic sense so this cannot, in any way, be described as representative sample of the population at large. For one thing, it was composed entirely of people that I liked and who liked me! And this was because I knew that they would give me the time and attention I needed. The purpose of these interviews was to give me sufficient data to come to some workable hypotheses that I could write about. They didn't let me down. My intuition tells me that their composite responses ring true. See what you think.

Our world is divided into three types of people; those we like, those we are indifferent to and those we positively dislike.

## People we like

I found that there is one overarching feature of the people we find likeable; these people show that they value us. They affirm us as unique human beings who have intrinsic value. Three factors of likeability sit together under this umbrella. The first relates to trust – we like people we can trust and also people who show that they trust us. This reflects the reciprocal nature of relationships. The second factor is also about the two-way nature of relationships – we like people who like us. And the third is seated in our innate selfishness – we like people who make us feel good. This sounds so simple but the complexity is revealed when we start to unpack these three factors.

### We like people who are trusting and trustworthy

Above all, we like people who are both trusting and trustworthy. The people we really like are invariably people in whom we can place absolute trust. We are pretty sure these people will not let us down. This shows itself in their ability to keep confidences and in their honesty and reliability. We can trust them with our secrets; we know they will be honest in their dealings with us and we are sure we can rely on them to carry out their promises to us. We know where we are with them because their words match their deeds. They give us no reason to doubt them or even to question their conduct. They are wysiwyg people (what you see is what you get) and there is no guile. That is not to say that they are necessarily easy to get to know. It may take us some time to realise that they possess these qualities – but when we get to know them we will find that they are open, honest, reliable. We both like and admire them for these qualities.

The difference between 'like' and 'admire' becomes apparent when we consider the two-way nature of relationships and trust. We admire people for their strengths. Admiration is rational and unidirectional and we may not even know the person we admire. We *like* people for both their strengths and their weaknesses. Liking is both rational and emotional and tends to be reciprocal. This difference between liking and admiring is thrown into sharp relief by the other side of the 'trustworthy' coin. We may not necessarily admire them but we certainly tend to like people who trust us – especially if that trust is sufficiently strong to allow them to share their vulnerabilities with us. Perhaps we like them because we recognise that we too are vulnerable and that we share humanity with all its frailties. Whether or not we see this in ourselves, we find it hugely likeable when people trust us to this degree for, in opening their areas of vulnerability to our gaze, they are taking an enormous risk. They are doing us the great honour of trusting us with their failings, their feelings and their self-esteem. If we are worthy recipients of that trust we will respect it and respond appropriately – but in addition, unbidden by us, this degree of trust brings an emotional response which can increase the bond between us.

In order for us to be able to consciously exhibit our shortcomings and vulnerabilities to others, we must have self-confidence; we need to have a good understanding of ourselves and to like what we see.  It also helps if we have the ability not to take ourselves too seriously – it's difficult to be pompous and share your vulnerabilities at the same time!   And of course we must have confidence in those with whom we entrust our weaknesses.  The benefit in trusting others in this way is that we enhance the bond of friendship between us.  The downside is that this can go badly wrong if our trust is misplaced.  We'll return to that later.

## We like people who like us

I've said that liking tends to be reciprocal – we are inclined to like people who like us.  Why should this be?  Well, by showing that they like us they are affirming us as valuable human beings, they are bolstering our self-esteem and they are fulfilling our need for affiliation.  In the presence of all these benefits, it would be churlish of us not to reciprocate!  But, how do we know that people like us?  Such is our problem with consciously interpreting the ambiguous signals we receive that we often don't pick up the vibes.  This is so prevalent that it is the stock in trade of romantic fiction.  We all know the age-old formula; boy meets girl, love puts an emotional charge in the air, girl misinterprets the signals, boy misinterprets the response, relations cool.  But, after all, this *is* fiction, so fate takes a hand and it all comes right for a happy ending.  The prejudiced Miss Bennett always falls into the arms of her proud Mr Darcy and we all breathe that collective sigh – Aaahh!  Perhaps we could produce more happy endings and fewer missed opportunities in real life if we understood the signals which people transmit when they like us.

To begin with, they will exhibit the opposite behaviour to that quoted in chapter 1.

If they like you:

They will give you more of their time and attention.

They will take more notice of what you say.

They will be more tolerant of your shortcomings and failures.

They will be more prepared to acknowledge your strengths.

They will give less weight to your weaknesses.

They will be more prepared to assist you.

And they don't go out of their way to avoid you. Quite the opposite, they will make efforts to be in your company.

At the receiving end, we may not realise that, for instance, we are getting more than our fair share of someone's time and attention. We don't know how they apportion their time. But while we are with them we need to be better at interpreting the verbal and non-verbal signals we receive. People who like us are likely to joke, have fun and, in particular, to tease us. They'll be relaxed and comfortable in our company and this is usually exhibited in slower speech patterns, more silences and a lowered tone of voice. It may also have the opposite effect in that the relaxation of inhibition may make them more lively and enthusiastic in their speech and actions. Their facial expression will be more inclined to a smile and what they don't say in words will be evident in their eyes. They are likely to make more eye contact and when they do there will be a softness of expression in their eyes which is present only when positive emotion is also present. They may also touch us more frequently than is their norm. Our interpretation and response to body language is usually subliminal so becoming conscious of people's non-verbal signals can be highly unnerving – be prepared! We return to this in chapter 4.

The key factor in the reciprocal response of liking people who like us lies in this feeling of being comfortable with them. This sense of ease in their company might be based on a variety of instances of 'sharing'. It could be shared interests – perhaps a hobby or pastime; shared values – having similar views on life; shared history – and this may be either having known each other for a long time or having been through a difficult time together. The sharing might also be that you are of a similar intellectual level or are taking similar routes on life's journey – possibly through work. Whatever the basis of this commonality, the outcome is that we find them easy to be with and easy to talk to. We have something in common which forms a bond about which we can talk. We can also share companionable silences with them. In a world where we have more than enough confrontation and aggravation in our daily lives, is it any wonder that we seek out people with whom we can be at ease?

## We like people who make us feel good

We like people who make us feel good about ourselves – people who lift our spirits. And they don't do this simply by being jolly.

'I can't understand why we get along so well'

They do it by exhibiting a generosity of spirit which appeals to our innate selfishness. We are drawn to them because they enrich our lives by showing care, consideration and affection towards us and they show their gratitude to us when we reciprocate. They listen to us. They laugh at our jokes. They are sensitive to our moods. They do not judge us but they show, by the way they respond to us, that they value us for the people we are. And because they are positive, optimistic, happy people they spread happiness wherever they go. They are attractive not because of their outward appearance but because of their inner qualities. And to cap it all, they are good fun.

Fortunately for us all, to be likeable you do not have to be a paragon of virtue. We may admire faultless people (or those whose weaknesses are hidden from us) but we like our people to come with imperfections. This is another aspect of 'making us feel good' as we compare ourselves with our friends and we don't come out too badly! It certainly makes people more user-friendly if they have faults – especially if they understand their faults and try to minimise their effect on us.

It seems that we are pre-programmed to like people until we are proved wrong. (All of my interviewees found it very easy to think of people they liked and extremely difficult to think of any that they disliked.) We also tend to like people who are liked by our friends. In this case, we are primed by people we like and prepared to take a positive view of a new acquaintance.

## Flipping the coin

This is not the full picture. Our feelings can change over time. Our initial likes may change to strong dislikes and vice versa. The change from like to dislike is dealt with more fully later and relates primarily to breaches of trust. For the change from dislike to like, we sometimes take an immediate dislike to a person and are proved wrong over time. When this happens, it is probably our intuition playing tricks. In order to help us make sense of the world we automatically categorise objects and people to fit them into memory. On first meeting, we subconsciously match people against our internal database of previous encounters with supposedly similar people and judge accordingly. So there are bound to be initial problems if our new acquaintance reminds us forcibly of sadistic Uncle Vernon; that same Uncle Vernon whom we still hate with the intensity of a neutron bomb because he was so unutterably cruel to us in our youth. It would take Mr New Acquaintance some time to get over that hurdle and become likeable in our terms; especially as we may not even realise that we are making this comparison! On further acquaintance, we may come to realise that the traits that we have attributed earlier are either not present or are more than counterbalanced by likeable traits, and so we change our minds. Of course, our initial feelings will remain unchanged if our instinct was spot on and Mr NA turns out to be Uncle Vernon re-incarnated. We will then continue to dislike him and do our utmost to avoid him.

## People we are indifferent to

The people we don't like fall into two distinct categories; those we are indifferent to and those we positively dislike. The great majority will fall into the first group. These people don't stand out; they have made little or no impression on us and we can take them or leave them. We haven't seen in them a sufficient number of likeable or dislikeable traits for us to reassign them to either of those categories. We haven't discovered much in common and probably haven't made efforts to do so. If we have tried to find common ground in shared interests or goals, we have been disappointed. There is no emotional engagement. We're here – they're here – and that's all. They are peripheral to our lives and unless we or they find reason for changing that non-relationship, they will remain so. We will continue to be ships that pass and re-pass in the night.

# People we dislike

We tend to either like or be indifferent to people until given reason to dislike them.

But, for each of us, there is a small group of people that we very emphatically dislike. And the overarching reason for our dislike is that these people share one fundamental characteristic – they damage other people. Whether by accident or design, they leave a trail of human destruction in their wake – and this can be on a small or large scale. Our dislike is very much more marked if the damage is caused to us or ours; if it is personal. Dislike also escalates with degree of damage. At the extreme, the people we dislike will exhibit all of the following characteristics; they will be selfish and manipulative and also bullying, untrustworthy, self-important, mean, prejudiced, and insensitive to their effect on others. In addition, if you need more, they will probably be unaware that they exhibit these traits. They rewrite history and don't face reality – well, certainly not the same reality as ours. This fits perfectly with the preservation of self-esteem. Let's face it – would any of us want to recognise ourselves from that description? And here's the rub – and a couple of questions for us all. Do other people see *any* of these traits in us? And do we *really* want an honest answer?

Grouping all those characteristics together has produced a caricature – a composite of all the dislikeable traits I have so far discovered. I have only once had the misfortune of working with someone who perfectly fitted this caricature. He was selfish and manipulative, a bully, he lied constantly and he was mean, prejudiced, and insensitive. The people who worked for him found him thoroughly obnoxious, and the taint of his behaviour and attitudes contaminated the working environment to such an extent that it became a very unhappy place to work. Luckily for me, I was able to make a hasty exit. Others were not so fortunate. It is comforting to know that there are not many in his league.

21

However, all of the people disliked by my interviewees exhibit one or more of these traits and the degree of dislike escalates with the number of dislikeable traits present and how much they affect us personally. So let's examine these traits and consider their effect on us as recipients.

## We dislike people who are manipulative

People who are manipulative use people and situations to their own advantage. They are always looking for gain for themselves – at the expense of others. They indulge in power play. They seem to enjoy playing people off against each other or latching on to others' weaknesses and using these to their advantage. They are highly competitive and will walk over anyone in order to climb the greasy pole. Thus, people become their victims, because manipulative people are looking for a win/lose outcome and they know how to ensure that they are on the winning side. They use power without responsibility – and this may be official power or their sexuality or any skill, ability or relationship which gives them a lever. We may merely disapprove of their behaviour until it damages someone we care about. Then the emotional reaction kicks in and disapproval turns immediately to dislike.

## We dislike bullies

The abuse of power takes another form when the power relationship puts a bully into the powerful position. Where the manipulative are usually motivated by a form of greed, bullies are motivated by anger and jealousy. Bullies channel their anger and aggression into behaviour which undermines others. This can take many forms. Public put-downs, sarcasm, personal criticism and destructive feedback are some of the explicit forms of bullying. But more subtle and invidious means of undermining confidence are also used. Encouraging malicious rumours, moving the goalposts, setting unreasonable expectations and goals are all features of bullying behaviour. There is sometimes a cruelty and malevolence in bullying that is awful to witness and is certainly destructive to both bully and bullied. As onlookers, we are embarrassed when we witness this type of behaviour. If we or our friends happen to be victims, our embarrassment turns to acute dislike.

## We dislike people we cannot trust

We also take a strong dislike to people we find untrustworthy – but again, disapproval only turns to dislike if there is a personal impact. This probably explains why we fail to dislike the rogues we see in the media. Their duplicity has not impacted specifically on us or on those we care about. Personal distrust and consequent dislike relates to both honesty and reliability and may either result from one incident or from an entire pattern of behaviour. Having placed our trust in someone, we react strongly when that trust is abused. Just one instance of breach of trust is sufficient for us to reverse our opinion; someone we liked becomes someone we positively dislike. This is particularly acute if there is hurt or pain or deep emotional attachment involved. The greater the damage caused by the abuse of trust, the greater the degree of dislike. Hence marital infidelity can score Hurricane Force 12 on an emotional reaction scale. At the other extreme, failure by someone to meet a deadline which causes us embarrassment may cause us brief annoyance but will not register long-term. However, repeated failures will accumulate; continued unreliability which causes aggravation to us eventually has an emotional impact.

In addition to the one-off breach of trust or continued unreliability, there is a pattern of behaviour which results in continued dishonesty. There are people who are terminally dishonest. These range from people who find truth an alien concept – those who are, in the words of one of my interviewees 'as straight as a corkscrew' – to those who simply bend the truth to suit their ends. They may be plausible for a time but once we have twigged that they are deceiving us, we will not only cease to believe them but will also begin to dislike them. The dislike stems from feelings of hurt, disappointment, embarrassment that we have allowed ourselves to be duped. Our self-perception as a 'good judge of character' has suddenly taken a nose dive.

This dishonesty may take the form of lies by commission or omission. They may change the story to suit the occasion or tell us what they think we want to hear. Or they may withhold vital information from us, ie. only tell us what they want us to know. The difference between this form of deception and 'white lies' rests with the motivation for each. The motive we attribute to people we choose to dislike is selfishness. We see their actions as solely servicing their own benefit with no concern for any possible damage to us. As with other dislikeable traits, we can see that it is me, me, me who takes precedence over anyone else and winning is the aim. It is unclear whether these people realise (a) that they are being dishonest, and (b) the effect their dishonesty has on others. Self-delusion can mask uncomfortable reality to such an extent that truth becomes transient and loses any vestige of constancy. For some people, truth is infinitely variable and telling what others would consider lies becomes a habit that is difficult to break. Sometimes their motivation in bending the truth is that they wish to be seen as likeable but the result is ultimately the opposite. When we find them out, we feel foolish, we feel angry, we feel conned and we dislike them for making us feel this way. So, it seems that, for anyone who doesn't want to be disliked, the maxim 'honesty is the best policy' would be a good one to adopt.

## We dislike people who are overly self-centred

We take a more mild dislike to people who are self-important, pompous, prejudiced or judgmental ie those people of fixed and firm opinions who will not listen to alternative views. These people are rather puffed up with their own very great importance. They tend to conduct conversations in the form of a monologue. If we can get a word in, and this could take some doing, it is immediately dismissed. Our words are of no consequence. This self-important behaviour is yet another form of selfishness. It is evident that these people value their own opinion above all others. In placing no value on the thoughts and perceptions of other people, they exhibit to the world that they also place little value on the owners of those thoughts and perceptions. None of us likes to feel undervalued, so the outcome is that we avoid them if we can. If we are confident of our opinions and have high self-esteem we can easily rationalise the dissonance and there will be little or no damage to our self-confidence, so the dislike will be mild. The emotional reaction will be greater if our self-confidence is already a little wobbly or if this person is a superior at work – both these instances will allow greater damage to our self-esteem and hence greater dislike.

## We dislike people who are mean

Just as we find generosity of spirit likeable, its opposite, meanness, is not a likeable characteristic. We view it with distaste. We will either dislike or feel sorry for people who are small-minded or avaricious – depending on the level of our feelings of generosity towards them. Because dealing with them leaves a sour taste, we will do what we can to avoid their company.

## We dislike people who are insensitive

We also have a degree of dislike for people who cause damage through their insensitivity. Because we assign meaning and motive to behaviour, we tend to be more forgiving of people who are insensitive. We can see that the damage is not caused by malice, selfishness or dishonesty but merely by ineptitude. That is not to say that insensitive people necessarily behave in a less destructive way than others we dislike. They can very effectively trample over the feelings of others and can leave just as great a trail of destruction as those who do so with purpose. Both in social situations and in the workplace, the sound of the clangers they drop can be deafening. They are completely unaware of the effect of their actions and their lack of empathy is outside their conscious

control.  We realise that there is no ill-will on their part and it is the lack of motive that makes the difference to our reaction.  People who cause embarrassment or hurt by insensitive behaviour do so because (a) they have not been able to put themselves in the shoes of the other person or (b) they have not picked up the verbal and non-verbal cues available to them, or (c) both of these.  They are missing some very important social and communication skills.  Depending on our disposition and the degree of damage to us, we may like them despite their insensitivity or dislike them because of it.

## Stereotyping

Disliking people because they damage us and ours is an emotional reaction but it is also a thoroughly rational and sensible thing to do.  But we are also inclined to take irrational dislikes to others.  In the same way that we matched Mr New Acquaintance to evil Uncle Vernon and perceived real or imaginary similarities, so we categorise and stereotype whole groups or races of people and decide we dislike them. This is another outdated survival mechanism. In our evolutionary past, we had to dislike the invading hordes – it was a case of kill or be killed. The other tribes were trying to damage us. It's not quite like that these days but our brains haven't yet evolved to meet this new reality.

## Some questions

All these findings have raised several questions in my mind. I just hope they are the same questions as yours!

How does being disliked relate to being successful? Certainly we all know of thoroughly dislikeable public figures who have risen to the top like the fat on the gravy – and were successful – for a time. But what happens long-term? On their rise to fame, they will have made many enemies and few friends. So, when an error is found (and which of us never makes a mistake?) and there is the inevitable reckoning, no-one steps forward to help or defend them. People will either stand aside and watch the humiliation with glee or join the back-stabbing in retaliation for past hurt. I can think of at least one British Prime Minister whose fall from power took this form.

We know that liking is reciprocal, so what about disliking? Unless the reason for our dislike of a person is due to their insensitivity, they will probably have picked up our non-verbal signals. Knowing, or even suspecting, that they are disliked is likely to damage their self-esteem, particularly if the person who dislikes them highlights their inadequacies or is a high status person. So we may find ourselves being disliked because, through no fault of our own, we make them feel bad about themselves. Their view of reality will be very different from ours.

And the big question for me relates to our differing views of reality. In most cases, those who are so heartily disliked by my interviewees have no inkling that this is the case. Consequently, they are also unaware of the reasons for that dislike. And even if they know, their self-protecting mechanisms will be working to try to prevent them from admitting that they exhibit traits that are dislikeable. I am being honest when I say that the last time I *know* for certain that my actions damaged someone was many years ago. I was working with a good friend and, through sheer thoughtlessness, I sent information to others while bypassing her. I knew she should be party to the information and I also knew that she was feeling vulnerable at the time. And it is her vulnerability which is the key to her reaction. It was an insensitive act on my part – but not a huge error. However, it hurt her deeply and it ended our friendship for ever. Since then, I've been rather more careful but I still don't *know* that I've been successful. That big question is 'How do we know whether we exhibit traits that make us dislikeable?' And I don't think I have the answer.

## Thinking time

Here are some questions which might help you discover some answers for yourself. This is not a test and there's no good or bad score. The purpose of these questions, and the ones that appear at the end of chapters 4,5,6,7 and 8, is to get you thinking about how you can increase your chances of getting on – both in your career and with other people. In their entirety, the chapter endings are designed to assist you to manage those opposites – fitting in, and standing out from the crowd. All these questions are reproduced at the end of the book in the section 'Questions, questions' so that you can, if you want, get some friends to help you.

Likeable traits are all related to valuing people

*1. Are you trustworthy?*

To think about: Trustworthiness is really important because it and its opposite feature highly in people's likes and dislikes. People who are discreet, honest and reliable are good friends and if you want to have good friends, you will need to be a good friend. We spent most of our waking hours at work so making and keeping good friends at work will make life much more productive and enjoyable.

Do you always keep secrets?

When people tell you some intimate or sensitive information about themselves, can they be sure that it will go no further?

Do you always tell the truth but try to do so in a way that ensures that damage to others is minimised?

Do you always try hard to fulfil your commitments to others?

If you are unable to keep your promise, do you tell people in good time?

Would people describe you as a good friend to have?

Would people describe you as trustworthy?

### *2. Are you trusting?*

To think about: On the whole, people live up to our expectations of them but, on occasion, they let us down. So, there will be breaches of trust. That's life. It takes both self-confidence and confidence in others to trust others with your weaknesses and vulnerabilities. But if you do, the emotional impact on the recipient of your trust will be substantial. If that person is worthy of your trust it will build a bond that will be difficult to break.

Do you trust people until you have reason to do otherwise?

Do you share both your strengths and your weaknesses with the people you trust?

Do you share your real vulnerabilities with the people you trust implicitly?

Would people describe you as trusting?

### *3. Do you show that you like people?*

To think about: We all get so confused by ambiguous signals – and we all give out ambiguous signals. Being more direct in your approach but also thoughtful about the impact – you don't want to frighten the horses – could make life so much more simple. (This will be explored further in Ch 4).

Do you tell people, in words of one syllable, that you like them?

When you are with people you like, do you give them your full attention?

Do you go out of your way to help them?

Do you joke with them and tease them?

Do you show that you are relaxed and comfortable in their company?

Do you smile at them, with both your lips and your eyes?

Do you touch them? (This is also further considered in Ch 4)

### 4.   *Do you make people feel good about themselves?*

To think about:  It is so easy to get caught up in the millions of tasks that we all have to undertake and to forget the little things which can bring joy to others.  Just remembering to thank them or asking about their new car, their child's exams or their holiday in Slovenia (remembering where they went gets you bonus points!) will make people feel that you value them.  Of course, if you're not really interested – then you shouldn't bother asking.

Tough one this!  Do you show care and consideration towards both the people you like and those you don't like?

Do you really listen to people?  A test – after they have gone, can you remember what they have said?

Are you sensitive to others' moods and change your behaviour to suit?

Do you resist the urge to pass judgement on others?

Do you forgive them for their flaws?

Do you show your gratitude for their acts of kindness?

Would people describe you as kind and considerate?

Are you positive, optimistic and happy – and do you spread happiness wherever you go?

Are you fun to be with?

And lastly for this section:

Do you know yourself well enough to be able to answer these questions?

To think about: Even if you do know yourself well, your perception of yourself will not be the same as others' perception of you. It is worthwhile asking a few trusted friends for their views.


Dislikeable traits are all related to causing damage to other people. It is hard to admit to any of these – but remember, nobody's perfect. Just look through to see if any of the questions raise doubts in your mind.

### 1. Are you selfish and manipulative?

To think about: This is an area it is difficult to own up to but, if you have always been encouraged to be competitive, especially in your childhood, it is easy to fall into the trap of habitually putting yourself first. You may think that win/lose is the only option available to you. Becoming more co-operative and less competitive will not be easy – but the benefits of moving from win/lose to win/win are considerable – and well worth the effort. Be aware though – if you have always been competitive, people will question your motives for a change in behaviour.

Do you cause or encourage conflict between people?

Do you use other people for your own advantage?

Do you look for weaknesses in others and use these against them?

Do you use your strengths as levers to gain advantage over

others?

Do people become your victims?

Do you look for a win/lose outcome?

Would people describe you as competitive?

Would people describe you as selfish?

Would people describe you as manipulative?

### 2. Are you a bully?

To think about: We have all heard of out-and-out bullies who make life unbearable for others. With malicious purpose, they set out to destroy the confidence of their victims. But what of the rest of us? We can, all of us, unwittingly be the perpetrators of bullying behaviour. You may think your sarcastic comments or put-downs are funny. To the recipient, they are certainly not funny, and to the audience, they are often embarrassing. Bolstering your confidence by belittling others will rebound on you and will win you no friends, just enemies. Bolstering the confidence of others by kind and helpful comments will have the opposite effect – and the rebound will be positive for your confidence too.

Do you administer public put-downs?

Do you use sarcasm?

In giving negative feedback, do you criticise the person not the action?

Do you gossip about people in an unkind way behind their backs?

Do you encourage malicious rumours and gossip?

Do you set unreasonable goals with the expectation that they will not be reached?

### 3. Are you untrustworthy?

To think about: It can take just one instance of indiscreet, dishonest or unreliable behaviour for trust to be lost completely – especially if the recipient is already feeling vulnerable. Once trust is lost, it is very difficult to regain. Prevention is so much better than cure.

Have you ever betrayed a confidence?

Have you ever betrayed someone's trust in you?

Have you ever told a lie to get yourself out of trouble?

Have you ever told a lie which hurt or damaged someone else?

Have you ever withheld information so that the person who needed that information was disadvantaged?

Have you ever let someone down because you could not fulfil a commitment you had entered into?

Would people describe you as indiscreet?

Would people describe you as dishonest?

Would people describe you as unreliable?

### 4. Are you self-centred?

To think about: Again, not easy to own up to, but sometimes we just take life too seriously. This trait can be lessened by taking a more relaxed attitude to life in general. Accepting that everyone has faults makes it easier to be kind to them. The next step is to forgive both ourselves and others because we all have shortcomings.

Do you take yourself too seriously?

Do you either ignore or refuse to listen to other peoples' points of view?

Do you undervalue the views of others?

Do you judge other people and find them wanting?

Would people describe you as self-important and pompous?

Would people describe you as prejudiced and judgmental?

Would people describe you as self-centred?

### 5. Are you mean?

To think about: It may just be thoughtlessness but ungenerous behaviour does rankle with people.

Are you overly concerned with money and possessions?

Do you get bound up in small and unimportant details causing others to become annoyed?

Are you always the last person to buy your round in the pub?

Would people describe you as small-minded?

Would people describe you as avaricious or mean?

### 6. Are you insensitive?

To think about: This is an area where you really can't answer for yourself and will have to ask others. Look at the questions on page 115 to give you something to reflect on.

Would people describe you as insensitive?

## chapter three

# Our world

## ...where we're going

So far, we've been thinking about ourselves and the effect we have on the world about us. By the exercise of careful choice about how we want to be, each of us, in our small way, can change our world, and our career chances, for the better. But first we must understand the changes that affect us at work and how best we can adapt to meet and greet today's and tomorrow's world. There is a growing consensus that in the present and future workplace, it will be the nice, smart people who will survive and prosper. Co-operation not competition is the name of the game. So, what is changing in our world that makes this a reality?

## The changing workplace

It is not by chance that governments throughout the world are focusing on their education systems. In a global economy it is the countries which adapt most successfully to future needs which will gain or retain prosperity. Precisely the same is true at a personal level. Those people who can predict and adapt to future work trends will be the ones who will survive and prosper.

### Communication

One can only marvel at the increased speed and volume of communication. Effective communication seals a relationship and oils its wheels. These days, we have one-way, two-way and many-way communication available 24/7. The nature and style of communication is changing in significant ways. Today, for most of us, face-to-face communication forms the minority of our interactions. This has two important effects. (1) It increases interaction while reducing the feeling of being connected. And (2) it ensures that most of the non-verbal cues which aid understanding are lost. So, for the vast bulk of our interactions, part of the human relationship has disappeared and we have available to us only a small part of the original information. No wonder interpretation of incoming messages has become so difficult. This wouldn't be such a problem if humans were adept at correctly interpreting the meaning behind people's words. But we're not! Miscommunication is rife because we each interpret information in relation to our prior knowledge, both of ourselves and of the sender. We'll return to this later but, to put it bluntly, communication from those people we like will get a far better reception than communication from those we don't.

## Attention

The increasing importance of attention has already been recognised in some sectors. Advertisers now talk about 'the attention economy' and children are increasingly being diagnosed as having 'attention deficit disorder'. Attention is in short supply. It is not that we all have less attention to give – merely that more people want a part of it. We are bombarded by people wanting to grab and hold our attention. Advertisers continually look for innovative ways to capture this precious commodity. Those employed in advertising and marketing are now putting even greater emphasis on building relationships with customers and engaging their emotions. They know that this will give competitive advantage in the shortage area of 'attention'. These are clever people. We should take note.

Attention is at a premium because our brains actively filter out the information which we do not want to notice. In order to ensure that our brains don't get overloaded, most of the signals which reach our senses are removed before they ever have a chance to enter our conscious minds. Those that get through are the ones that are pertinent because they carry high value for us. One set of high value messages are those that are carried by people of high value to us – people we like. On a cold cost analysis, marketing and advertising can cost megabucks, but a smile or a friendly word, or any signal that shows that you are interested in people, costs absolutely nothing. The personal touch remains a very potent way of gaining someone's attention and we all have the personal touch. People who are already in a positive relationship are at an advantage in gaining each other's attention. The nature of relationships may change but, whatever their nature, there remains at their core a thread which binds participants. I call that thread 'likeability'. You may have a different name for it.

## Customer expectations

Customers are becoming more discerning. At work, we all have customers. Most organisations now consider themselves to have both internal and external customers; these being anyone for whom we, as employees, provide a service. It used to be sufficient to provide an efficient service. Today, this is the absolute minimum. In a world competing for customer attention and subsequent business, the stakes have been raised. We now have organisations which declare that their customers will be 'thrilled' and 'delighted'. We have entered a world of excess in customer satisfaction. The use of these superlatives has raised expectations and the people we serve are beginning to expect to be delighted rather than merely satisfied. They expect efficiency plus an added mystery ingredient. Dealing with someone they like could be just what they are looking for.

## The nature of work

The nature of work, where we do it, how we do it and for which employer, is changing. Today, we operate in an information economy, we form part of a globally networked society, we trade in a borderless world and we work – where do we work? We are in

'Huh! You think **you've** got a complaint. Just thank your lucky stars
you don't have to work here!'

danger of working everywhere and all the time.

- In the Western world manufacturing jobs have greatly reduced
  and service jobs are being exported to developing countries.
  The three main areas of growth in the developed world are in
  the hospitality, care and communications sectors. Employment
  in these sectors is set for further expansion. Each of these
  requires the employee to talk to the public and to have highly
  developed 'people skills'.

- Technological, economic and societal changes have led to an
  increase in self-employment, small business start-ups (many
  by women), teleworking (full or part time) and working from
  home. The delineation between private and working life is
  being eroded.

- The increase in the proportion of small businesses is partly
  the result of the waves of lay-offs during the 'right-sizing'
  (odious word!) which started in the 1980s and '90s and which
  continues still. The 'de-layered' have had to acquire new sets
  of skills in order to prosper as entrepreneurs.

- Long term career path planning is a thing of the past. Young workers today face the prospect of having several careers over their lifetime. For each career change, they must have the personal skills necessary to ensure that they are recruited, selected and retained by their next employer.
- The trend for companies to employ a small core workforce with satellite contractors looks set to continue.

For those employed, be it in a large or small organisation, in the public or private sector, the prospect of a job for life has gone. The psychological contract between employee and employer used to be that, as long as the employee gave good service, their job was pretty much guaranteed. The best employers today offer a different psychological contract to their staff. Here it is not employment that is guaranteed but employability. In return for good service, they offer continuous development of the employee to ensure that, when there is a parting of the ways, the employee is fit for the marketplace. Bad employers, and there are far too many of these, offer no such contract. It is left to their employees to ensure their own continued employability and professional development.

## Accepting the challenge

This could all become terribly depressing. This fast-evolving world provides huge challenges but it also offers real opportunities. You can either look at it in horror and retreat into your cave or relish the challenge it offers and go for it. Technology can either be friend or foe, increased expectations can lead you to excel or to resign yourself to mediocrity and the changing face of the workplace can provide the opportunity for you to find a better niche for yourself. It depends on your perspective; it is your choice.

There are, of course, external constraints which limit our choice, but most of our limiting factors come from within. They stem from our lack of faith in ourselves and our fear of the unknown. Those who will prosper in the future will be the ones who can recognise the difference between internal and external constraints and can overcome their own particular self-limiting factors.

# Evolution, revolution and a foray into physics

In our working lives we find ourselves at a point where so much is changing and so many of these changes are interacting that it can be difficult to see where it's all leading.

This is a practical book – it doesn't dwell on theory. And I'm not a physicist, but I have found three theories from physics that together shed some light on how the world works – and us too. These theories focus on 'systems' and the relationships created both within and between these systems.

**Complexity theory in two sentences:**

The universe is made up of complex adaptive systems. If you change one part of any of these systems you may get the expected results but there will also be unintended consequences.

**Chaos theory in two sentences:**

In complex systems the starting conditions have a huge effect on the outcome, so if you vary the starting conditions by a tiny (possibly undetectable) amount, you will get a completely different outcome. It's that butterfly's wing thing.

Note: The saying is that the beat of a butterfly's wing in China can cause a hurricane in America. Someone apparently tracked through all the possible effects of each stage of the changing air movements caused initially by the beat of those fragile wings.

**Quantum theory in two sentences:**

Quantum theory states that you cannot know the starting conditions completely. Combined with complexity and chaos theories this all means that there is no way that you can predict the future with any certainty.

This all suggests that we live in a world which is changing quickly and unpredictably. The changes are so many and so fast that it is easy to feel that it is all outside our control. It seems to me that this has four important lessons for us all:

1.   Values. In order to retain some element of control, it is vitally important that we are grounded in a strong set of personal values so that we are not blown off course.

2.   Adaptation. In addition, we need to be open to the possibility of a spectrum of different futures and sufficiently flexible to be able to adapt to a variety of new circumstances.

3.   You never know. Human beings are also complex adaptive systems so there will be both predicted and unexpected outcomes to all of our actions.

4.   Relationships. To retain stability in our lives, the need to build strong and lasting relationships will become increasingly important both at work and at home.

That all sounds good to me. Scary but good! It brings both problems and risks – but the opposite is far worse. Which of us would want to be bored to death in a totally predictable world?

The effect of all of these world and work-pattern changes is that wherever and however we are employed, be it self-employed, employed or employer, whether in a large or a small organisation, in the public or the private sector – we are all vulnerable. In order that we might overcome this vulnerability, there is an urgent need for each of us to regularly re-examine our skill set. But there is more. In order to ensure our survival and prosperity we must also have the ability to:

- get on with a vast array of people
- communicate in ways that gain influence
- constantly network
- continually market ourselves
- re-evaluate and refine our leadership capability and
- continually upgrade our skills and broaden our horizons.

In order to get on in our careers, we must make it a priority to fit in with the people we work with yet stand out from the crowd.  And there's a bonus:

We develop a strong group of friends and allies

We achieve our goals

We realise what's great about ourselves

We help others achieve and be successful

And it doesn't have to be staid and serious – it can be fun!

## chapter four

# Communicating

## ... with head and heart

If your goal is to get on with other people and get on in your career, then why, you might ask, is an understanding of human communication the key to success? The answer is simple. Communication is THE crucial factor in the development of relationships. Communication, both spoken and written, is all-pervasive – it is everywhere. It is so prevalent in our lives that it has become invisible to our gaze. We give little thought to its importance or the nature of its development. Yet the quality of our communication impacts dramatically on the quality of our relationships. We would do well to give it the attention it deserves.

## What is communication?

We think that we communicate with words – and we do. Words are central to our communicative skill but they form only a small part of our repertoire. We communicate in all that we say and do, and in all that we leave unsaid and undone. Every minute that we are in company we are involved in intentional or unintentional communication. And, in today's world, because we use written words and electronic communication, we continue to communicate for much of the time that we are alone. No wonder people call it the communication age. In all our face-to-face communication, we transmit verbal and non-verbal signals for other people's antennae to receive. Some are better than others at picking up these cues (fortune tellers and stage magicians are adept), but to a greater or lesser extent, in every encounter, we expose to the world elements of precisely who we are. And even when we communicate at a distance, our messages still impart knowledge about us that we did not intend.

To be so exposed can be a frightening prospect – but it need not be if we think of it in terms of our need for affiliation. It is fortunate for us that people are predisposed to liking each other – so we have to be pretty extreme in what we are, what we say and what we do, to be actively disliked.

We tend to forget that communication, just like relationships, is reciprocal; it is two-way (or many way). We listen and we speak; we read and we write, we take turns and we match each other's body language. We engage with each other in a dance of words. And words have power. Words have the power to harm or to heal – and once uttered, they cannot be retrieved. They take on a life of their own and they are received and understood in ways that we cannot fully predict.

# How is communication changing?

With the explosion in electronic communication, words have taken on even greater power. In emails, words are stripped bare; in text messages even more so. We cannot see the smile, we cannot hear the softness in the tone, we cannot feel the gentle touch on the arm. A whole range of non-verbal cues are missing and emoticons are a poor substitute :-( We receive too many emails and texts so we skim them briefly. We are in a hurry so we respond immediately. The conditions are ripe for miscommunication big time.

Why does this happen? It is because our primary senses for the receipt of communication are changing and we are ill adapted to cope with this change.

For thousands of years after humans developed the power of speech, our modes of communication remained stable. The coming of the printing press and the slow development of mass literacy produced a revolution. We are now in the middle of a second revolution. Before the development of written communication, all words were spoken. All communication was face-to-face. We primarily used hearing but also sight, touch and intuition to understand both the words and their context. We are now in retreat from face-to-face communication. We have letters, faxes, telephone, email, texting. We conduct the majority of our dialogues at a distance and often with people we have never met. With the exception of the telephone, we rely only on sight of the words and intuition to enable us to decode their messages. Most of the time this is not a problem and would never be – if we were Vulcans. A rational decoding of either spoken or written text would reveal the information message within. But we humans read so much more into the message. Our intuition brings prior knowledge to bear and we assign meaning far beyond the text. In addition, with or without our permission, our emotions become involved.

In this world of networked communication, speed is of the essence. And in our everyday encounters we are continually in a hurry. If we are not to fall into the trap of miscommunication and resultant damage, we need to understand both the basis of human communication and its power to build or destroy relationships.

## How does communication work?

The process of communication involves sending, receiving and interpreting messages. In the animal kingdom all five senses are used – and possibly sixth and seventh senses too. In moving up the evolutionary ladder, humans have lost much of the communicative power of taste and smell. This has some aesthetic benefits. (Ask yourself this – have you ever seen dogs shaking hands when they meet?) Of the five senses, most of human communicative power is concentrated in just three; sight, hearing and touch. We have a lesser understanding of our 'sixth sense' where the sense organ is not the eyes or ears but the brain. But we also use it in communication. This sense is sometimes called intuition, but goes under a variety of names; instinct, gut reaction, 'a feeling'. Intuition is the result of an analysis of our past experiences, conscious and unconscious.

Sight and hearing are complex but largely physiological processes. In each, the signals entering the brain are relatively unambiguous. But that doesn't prevent problems; interpretation by the brain is part of the process and each of these senses can be fooled. Our hearing can be fooled by 'Chinese whispers' and sleight of hand tricks get us every time. Touch has additional complexity in that it is a powerful communicator of emotion and thus it is hedged around with protocols and taboos. Our sixth sense again is different. Our intuition draws on the wealth of our past experience. Thus it should always be taken seriously but it is not without its problems. It relies on the workings of our memory and human memory is idiosyncratic. Both embedded memories and new signals can be ambiguous or contradictory or just plain wrong. Our hearing and sight can be tricked, even more so, our intuition. This plays the biggest tricks of all.

We saw an example of this with evil Uncle Vernon and Mr New Acquaintance. Our intuition tells us that these two are similar in some way so must be similar in others. Our rational minds know that this doesn't make sense – but our rational minds often don't get a look-in! It all happens subconsciously. And even when rational thought is involved, we have to make an effort to override our intuition. Here's an example where intuition could have led me up the garden path. My mother was a wonderful woman but she did have some odd ideas. She gave me a great deal of advice when I was young, including the stricture, 'Never trust a man with small hands'. I am consciously aware that I have internalised this message and can rationalise it and put it to one side – well, almost! Thirty years on, even though I know that there is absolutely no correlation between trustworthiness and hand size in the male population, I still instinctively look at men's hands when I first meet them. I just can't help myself. And then there's that small part of my brain saying, 'Don't trust him – he's got tiny hands!' Just as we shouldn't totally trust the evidence of our own eyes and ears, so we should question our intuition. Of all of our senses, this is the one most likely to skew the messages we receive so that they take on an entirely different meaning from the one intended.

Communication might seem like throwing and catching a ball but it's not that simple. It is more like throwing a dog and catching a cat. The message is similar – it still has four legs, a head and a tail – but, in transit, it has changed into a completely different animal.

## The verbal / non-verbal divide

Human communication is extraordinarily complex and infinitely variable. It is often quoted that communication is 20% verbal (the words we use) and 80% non-verbal (every other part of the

'I know you believe you understand what you think I said but I am not sure you realise that what you heard is not what I meant'

message). The truth behind the numbers is that, in any dialogue, the majority of the message we receive is *not* contained in the words. Our understanding of both the power and effect of our words is limited. We understand even less about the power and effect of our non-verbal messages. They are usually below our level of consciousness or outside our focus of attention which, of course, increases their power. Because they are outside our conscious control, our ability to rationalise them is limited, leaving our emotions to have a field day.

## Words, words, words

Let's think about words. They can ripple like a gently flowing stream; they can have charms to soothe the savage breast or they can whip up a storm; it depends how we use them. Single words don't make much sense – it is the way we combine them and the metaphors and analogies we use which carry the message. In writing the beginning of this paragraph, I tried and failed to use a war-like metaphor. I couldn't find combative words to describe what I wanted to say – but many people do. They talk of leading the troops, having someone in their line of fire and outflanking them. They look for chinks in their armour and decide to take people out – and they don't mean to dinner. The words we use say a lot about us. We should choose them with care.

The richness of the language we use increases its emotional impact. Bald messages giving straight information have their place; they fulfil their purpose and appeal directly to the head – our rational part. However, if we want to influence people or events – and which of us doesn't – our task is made easier if we can engage people's rational thought processes and their emotions; both head and heart. I would defy anyone to remain unmoved by this extract from an email from a young volunteer working in Africa:

> IM SOOOOO EXCITED! I'm so excited i cant tell u how excited i am. Let me explain so u don't think I'm a complete nutter!

Here's the background... its all about the vocational school that closed two years ago. I went to visit Lugoda-Lutali which is a village quite near to Utosi. And their primary school headteacher has been collecting statistics. Basically each year at least 28 out of the 30 girls that finish primary school go off to Iringa or Dar es Salaam as house girls. This really shocked me which is very silly of me because there are no young girls at all in Utosi cos they're all sent off as house girls, but you never really get your head around this sort of thing do u.

Then at our ward primary event we had a very moving speech from doctor Mbata who is an absolute legend. He is the head of Mafinga hospital which serves the whole district. He was saying how every day he sees many girls arrive at the hospital who have returned from Dar es Salaam. These girls all go straight to the hospital from the bus and die of AIDS there without ever making it back to their families. He talked about looking after all of these girls with AIDS until they finally die, without him ever knowing their names cos they are too ill to tell him. So the families never find out what happened to their child.

In Utosi at the moment the only option apart from becoming a house girl is to send the girls to the mission sewing school, which charges 60,000tsh. This is more than 3 times the average family's yearly income! Unsurprisingly no-one from Utosi actually goes there. So you can imagine my motivation is great for getting this vocational school going again. Anyway i hit a bit of a brick wall on the charities front. So i got myself all upset n worried n stuff n then had the most wonderful day. That's today! I've worked out everything required and got loads of quotes for prices and it's only gonna be 500 quid! So Julia and me, we're just gonna pay for it, and set up a link with two charities for any future costs. HOORAY!

This is the best news ever ever ever! I can't tell u what a brilliant day i'm having, and i cant wait to tell the headmistress cos she'll be so excited. She absolutely loves the kids at her school and she's been trying to get the vocational school going again ever since it closed. Fancy it only costing 500 quid! HOORAY! I'm extremely emotional at the mo so there's all sorts of happy and sad crying going on, but today it's all happy.

Love you all

Sian

The content captures emotion but, in addition, the use of words and sentence structure cause emotion to spring from the page. You can feel the excitement, the sadness, the anger and the joy. The construction also draws on the age-old tradition of story telling. Throughout human history, stories have been used to pass on traditions, to convey lessons and to elicit emotions. In our society, the oral tradition of story telling is alive and well on stage and screen. The written tradition of fictional books is thriving. There is something in the human psyche which leads us to enjoy stories and telling a story is an exceptionally good way of communicating. And by the way, this story has a happy ending. She managed to get the vocational school reopened and running. She's my daughter and I'm so proud of her!

The moral of this story: We can all do great things – greater than we ever thought possible – if we have the determination to succeed.

The moral of telling a story: A tug at the heartstrings – especially at work, where it is unexpected – can have huge impact. It is potentially very powerful so choose carefully how you do it.

Words used to be ephemeral – sometimes remembered by those who heard them and sometimes not. Today, they can easily come back to haunt us. Our spoken words are often recorded and our written words form a permanent record of our thoughts at any juncture. The current speed of communication means that we now produce more words and we produce them in a hurry. A pause to consider the effect of our words on both our intended and unintended audiences could serve to strengthen our relationships. Well chosen words can bind us more closely to the recipient. They can also save us a great deal of trouble.

To go back to the cat and dog metaphor (with apologies to animal lovers); if we toss our greyhound around for a while before throwing it, it might at least arrive as a wolfhound – a different shape of hound, but a hound none the less.

If we think words are problematic then it is without doubt that non-verbal communication is a minefield (a war-like metaphor!)

## Non-verbal signals

If you want to expose yourself to an array of non-verbal signals, then go to a public meeting conducted in a language you don't understand. My purpose in attending such a meeting was to improve my French. Fat chance of that – I very quickly lost the plot. But that left me free to watch and listen to the different speakers without having to concentrate on the words. I noticed the tone of voice and the modulations in pitch, the speed and clarity of delivery, the facial expressions, the hand movements and the body language. I also took in the amount of eye contact offered and returned.

Oh dear, oh dear. There were six presenters, but only one managed to forge any sort of relationship with the audience. She did this by using the non-verbal part of her message to underscore her words. She spoke slowly and with clarity and she enunciated well. She varied her speed and pitch, and used pauses to emphasise some of her words. She smiled – gently and often, she offered eye contact, she showed the palms of her hands and she stood straight and tall. And how do I know she gained rapport with her audience? Because their body language told me so. They leaned forward, they focused their eyes on her, they smiled and nodded as she spoke and when she had finished, they gave her a standing ovation.

She had engaged both their rational thought processes and their emotions – and with the use of just two of our senses; sight and sound. No doubt it was the mixture of the words she used and the way she presented them which reached out and touched that audience – but touch them she did, if only metaphorically.

In those presentations physical touch was absent, but consideration of the communicative power of our sense of touch takes us into a completely different league. Touch gives out signals of the greatest magnitude – the most potent and therefore the most fascinating non-verbal messages of them all.

Touch is therapeutic. We all need to be touched. It is well documented that babies fail to thrive if they are denied touch and that depression in old people is relieved simply by including the briefest of touches in their daily routine. Touch is such a powerful communicator that, in normal circumstances, we choose to restrict our use of it. We touch each other most at times of heightened emotion – especially at times of great intimacy, joy or sorrow. At these times touch offers comfort, empathy, a sharing of the pleasure or the pain. Anger also engenders a greater degree of touch, but here the touch is neither gentle nor therapeutic!

Increased touching follows heightened emotions, but the sequence also works in reverse with the touch preceding the emotion. Our touch receptors are highly charged and when someone touches us, there is always an emotional response. Normally, without conscious thought, our brains rationalise that response to fit the circumstances. So, for instance, on a crowded train, we will not normally notice the touches from all around. The same touches on an empty train would certainly not be acceptable.

It is this immediate engagement of our emotions which makes

touch the dynamite of the non-verbal world. This, together with our understanding of the natural link between touch and intimacy has made us understandably wary of using it. Yet, in all relationships, whatever the degree of intimacy, touch can have an important role. Appropriate touching produces a pleasant response in the person touched and serves to cement and enhance a relationship. So, in order to include touching in our repertoire, but also to avoid charges of sexual harassment, we have ritualised our touching in the workplace. These rituals such as hand-shakes, pats on the back or even hugs also occur more frequently at times of increased intimacy, joy or sorrow.

The rituals differ between cultures but there are some global norms. Wherever we go in the world there are gender differences. Man/man touches differ in type and frequency from both woman/ woman touches and cross sex touches. And in all cultures it is usually the case that the higher status person initiates the touch. These stylised touches are also restricted to the areas of the body considered 'safe' in erotic terms.

I asked some male and female friends for their perspective on this. I asked when they felt it natural to touch in the workplace. Here are a typical male and female reply:

Me Mike, You Jane,

By way of background, I believe that most British males, certainly of my generation and probably still, are a bit reserved/ shy/anally retentive (joke that last one....or maybe not) and therefore don't touch more than they think the occasion demands – shaking hands when being introduced to someone they've not met before or whom they haven't seen for a while, or when they're saying goodbye to someone they won't be seeing for a time. So, I would shake hands with clients when saying hello or goodbye, new colleagues I was meeting for the first time and colleagues whom I hadn't seen or wouldn't be seeing for some time. The only other circumstances where I think it would be entirely natural to shake hands would be congratulations (well done on having got away with that huge tax fraud – how is the yacht by the way?), commiserations (bad luck on getting caught – when do you come up for sentencing?) and where it's the other person's custom to do so, eg the first hello in the day for a Frenchman.

99.9% of my touches would be handshakes (almost always one-handed), ie virtually no arm-pressing or embraces. The exception would be embraces for women, provided we both regarded each other as friends, re congratulations or commiserations. As for other touching, I suppose if the point of a joke were better made by touching the other person's thigh I would do so – but only if it would not cause alarm and, of course, only in the best possible taste.

As regards going beyond handshakes; I don't find it natural to embrace males unless there is a strong element of jokiness to it; when dealing with superiors, I would not do so unless we were extremely close friends; I don't think age in itself would be an issue, although I suppose I would err on the side of being more formal with people I regarded as much older or younger than me, ie if in doubt, don't make anyone feel uncomfortable.

The making people feel uncomfortable bit is probably the key to it all. I certainly wouldn't want to make the other person feel uncomfortable, nor would I want to feel uncomfortable myself – if in doubt, I would hope to be seen as more rather than less reserved. As for why all this should be, I can only say that it comes from how I was brought up – not the specific set of manners I learned but the general principles I think should govern how people deal with each other. Maybe I should get out more!

Love (but keeping my hands to myself), Mike

and from an older female person's perspective:

> In a working context, I find that I tend to offer support by a little pat on the shoulder at the back (shoulderblade?) or leaving the hand on the back for a little while. And it is a supportive / encouraging / haven't you done well thing, particularly for men or women who are uncertain or new to their role. It is slightly motherly I think but not confined to younger people. It also says 'I value and support this person'. Sometimes it is an affectionate gesture between perceived equals. I think you might also find it in older men bosses acting in a mentoring capacity? It may also be interpreted as shoving someone into the breach!!! (get in there my son!) Also I guess, it is highly non-sexual – being on the back and high up and very light.
>
> There is another action – shoulder to shoulder side on which sort of indicates – 'We're in it together' – between equals I think. A dig / pressure arm to arm means 'Hey look at that!'
>
> Arms round waist or ribs is 'all girls together'
>
> I really don't like people holding on to my hand, double handed shake or touching my lower arm or elbow – feels calculated, smarmy and insincere to me – but then I have read the articles about how to come across as warm and sincere!
>
> Diana

These are British examples and it has to be said that the British as a race are more 'out of touch' than most other cultures. And, of course, this cultural divide can, itself, cause miscommunication.

But, wherever you are, the link with intimacy means that for any touch there is the potential for a sexual element. And this is true for both same sex and other sex touching. The reason that touch is such a potential disaster area is that this powerful emotional communicator gives out ambiguous signals. This combines with our propensity for misinterpreting the signals we receive and Hey presto! major problems. This is hugely regrettable because the benefits of touching are considerable. Touch enhances both our physical and mental well-being and the health of our relationships in all spheres of our lives including our work. In the changing workplace where boundaries between work life and private life are disappearing, we would do well to re-evaluate its place in our repertoire. But whatever place we decide for it, in order to avoid confusion, it is important to ensure that we always remain within the comfort zone of the recipient – and we do this by noticing their non-verbal response.

Although touch is the most powerful transmitter of emotion, our other senses are also travelling on this emotional bandwagon. The cumulative effect is that the signals we transmit produce a positive, neutral or negative emotional response. Emotions are contagious so the quality of our communication can have effects far beyond our intended audience. By communicating well, we can have substantial influence on the quality of our working environment.

So by our choice of words and, more importantly, by the non-verbal signals we give out we can produce a positive emotional response in people. Tell me, if you can, the difference between 'positive emotional response' and 'liking' because I can't see much between them.

## Improving your communication

To increase your chances of getting on at work, both by enlarging your sphere of influence and improving your working relationships, your communication should engage both head and heart. In order to encourage a positive emotional response you should make sure that your communications, whether face-to-face or at a distance, make people feel good about themselves. With just a little thought it is possible to engage the emotions of the recipient. You can do this by revealing your own emotions and by showing that you care about the other person. Your communications should always be honest but they should also be sensitive and you need to take notice of the response – it gives you vital clues as to how to proceed. Changing the tenor of your communications in such a way that it becomes clear that the recipient is important to you makes those communications more acceptable and consequently more effective.

# Thinking time

## Communicating

### 1. Do you communicate clearly?

To think about: Lack of clarity leads to so many miscommunications which, in turn, lead to misunderstanding and the potential souring of relations. With just a little thought, the clarity of your communications can improve dramatically.

In all your communications, spoken or written, do you ensure that there is complete understanding?

Do you summarise at intervals and ask for feedback to ensure clarity and mutual understanding?

Are you aware of the non-verbal signals you transmit?

Do your verbal and non-verbal signals give out the same message?

Would people describe both your written and spoken communications as clear and unambiguous?

### 2. Do you communicate with sensitivity?

To think about: We cannot know for certain how others will respond to our communications. However, some consideration of the possible impact will help to produce the effect you desire rather than some random effect over which you have no control.

Do you ensure that you communicate with the right people at the right time so that they all feel included and informed?

Do you consider the impact on the recipient of all your written and verbal utterances?

Do you choose your words carefully so as to ensure that they do not offend?

Would people describe your communications as sensitive?

### 3. Do your communications engage people's emotions?

To think about: If you want to have influence, then you must make your audience laugh, cry, smile, punch the air – or give any signal which tells you they are emotionally engaged. It also helps if what you say makes sense!

Do your communications tell a story?

Do you choose your words carefully so as to elicit positive emotions?

Do you use analogy and metaphor to increase the richness of your communication?

Do you expose some of yourself and your emotions in your communications?

Do you use non-verbal signals, especially eye-contact, smiling and touch to increase the emotional impact of your communication?

Would people say that they enjoyed receiving your communications?

### 4. Are your communications reciprocal?

To think about: We tend to concentrate on our side of the dialogue – the speaking and writing. But it *is* a dialogue – and listening and reading are probably of greater importance to us, because it is through these that we learn.

In your communications do you always ensure that there is the opportunity for dialogue?

Do you allow others to influence you?

Do you actively listen and read – and this means giving all of your attention – when others communicate with you?

Do you always respond when others contact you, even if only to say 'thanks but no thanks'?

Do you always respond in an encouraging and constructive way to the communications of others?

Would people describe you as a good communicator?

*Stand out - Fit in - Have fun*

## chapter five

# Networking

## ... going for win/win

We are all familiar with the saying 'It's not what you know, it's who you know'. But, it's no longer a question of one or the other; both will be vital for survival and prosperity. 'Who you know' will get your feet under the table. 'What you know' will ensure that you're still sitting at the table when the coffee and mints are served.

People who are self-employed, in a partnership or in a small business understand the importance of networks for gaining business. Word-of-mouth is vital for continued viability. In this environment, 'who you know' has a huge impact on the amount of work you get. Within large organisations, it is no different. In this environment also, word-of-mouth counts and networking has always been a primary means of advancement.

But we now have an added dimension. The workplace is becoming increasingly like the Mad Hatter's Tea Party. Even if you manage to keep your feet under the table throughout the meal, it is by no means certain where you'll be sitting at the end of it. If you haven't yet had to play mad musical chairs in a firm where a restructuring has meant that everyone has to apply for their own job, think yourself lucky – for the moment. The restructuring Tea Party is only one example of job change. We are also seeing an increase in takeovers, mergers and amalgamations and the exponential growth of some companies while others quickly fade. Don't kid yourself that in this environment 'what you know' will necessarily lead to promotion either within or outside your present workplace – or that it will even ensure that you keep your present job. Networking with the right people has a major part to play in your continued viability.

Some people are consummate networkers. They are like spiders at the centre of a web of contacts and they are continually expanding that web. All their actions have a networking aspect. These are the people we go to when we need a contact – because we know that if they don't know the answer, they'll know someone who does. And they thoroughly enjoy being the person who knows. They are the nodes in their networks. But not everyone can be or even wants to be a node. However, for all of us, it is well worthwhile to be part of at least one network which has an effective node.

## Official and unofficial networks

In less egalitarian times, networks were male-oriented and often clandestine. Men would meet to discuss business at the golf club

'I say old chap, I think I can put some work your way'

or via some secret society. The old boys' network worked behind the scenes to promote some and exclude others. It was largely the minority groups, women and ethnic minorities, who were excluded. The balance has been redressed somewhat, with minority groups forming their own networks, but it is by no means a level playing field yet.

Times are gradually changing and there is now a vast array of official networking opportunities. Networks have been set up for different interest groups, different sectors of society, on an international, national or regional basis. It is worth investigating these to see if there is mutual advantage in your involvement. In addition, conferences, exhibitions and away-days all create opportunities for official networking.

As important as these official networks are, it is often our unofficial networks which create the opportunities we need in order to advance our careers. It is the people we get on with socially – possibly through a shared interest – who will, most likely, be the ones who help us get on in our career. And email makes it so easy!

# Finding a new job

A great deal of headhunting is done through unofficial networks. Your friend in a rival firm will think of you when a suitable job comes up – a good friend will anyway! This has the added advantage that your current employer may be jolted into action by the realisation that you are employable elsewhere. It could be that you are forced to find a new job, and then your networks are a good place to start. Your contacts might not be able to help directly, but through their own networks, they may know someone who can.

# Keeping the job you have

Networks are not only useful for gaining new work but also for improving the quality of your current work. The people who form the connections in your networks can help you by providing technical expertise which is beyond your own capabilities and by mentoring (talking through problems), coaching (leading you through problems) and augmenting your knowledge base – the acknowledgements in this book are testament to this!

The link between getting on with people and networking is obvious. Will any of us want to spend time and energy making and maintaining contact with people we don't actually like? We may find that we have to for a time – but as soon as the primary reason for the contact is lost so will be the connection. But there is a pleasure in continuing contact with people we get on with, and we can happily mix business with pleasure. The benefit for us, if we are likeable, is that a variety of people will want to keep in contact with us. In our complex and chaotic world where the future is uncertain, we do not know what chance connection might just provide the opportunity we are looking for. Keeping all channels open to the people you like need not be time consuming and has the potential for both process and outcome benefit. You can enjoy the process and you may also reach some positive outcomes. But don't forget, you are looking for win/win outcomes. If you look for win/lose your network will soon disappear because high on the list of features people dislike are selfishness and manipulation.

It is not always plain sailing when you begin to enlarge your networks in a systematic way. Few of us find it easy to consciously extend and maintain our web of contacts. We are busy so don't get round to it; we are not confident that our approach will be welcome; we can't quite see the benefit for the people we are contacting. It's true – when you try to include new contacts in your networks, some people will not recognise the value of networking so will not respond. Others may not realise your value to their network and will also not respond. We know that people's time is precious and we do not want to intrude so it is sensible to concentrate on those whose reaction is positive. You must be confident that you can offer a reciprocal arrangement of some kind, but this does not have to be an equal partnership. You might ask yourself, why would people respond? Why would they put themselves out to help me in my present or future employment? The reason is simple. It is because networking is also fulfilling their needs. Networking is a reciprocal arrangement. This will manifest itself in both the rational and the emotional spheres. Rationally, they will need to be aware that you will reciprocate and will use your knowledge and networks to their advantage whenever you can. Furthermore, there is a 'matchmaker' in all of us, so there is a sense of achievement for them in engineering a win/win outcome. And for those who are in positions of authority there is the desire in them to pass on knowledge. And emotionally, they do it because they like you.

So, in a nutshell, how do you create and maintain these networks of relationships? By being the sort of person that others want to relate to and by using your excellent communication skills of course.

# Thinking time

## Networking

To think about: The very effective networkers spend much of their time networking. But they don't see it as a separate task. It is an integral part of all that they do. There is a networking strand in all their encounters and they constantly pick up and store information for later use – and they are always looking for win/win.

Do you make a habit of getting contact details from people you meet?

Do you make sure that you remember pertinent facts about them?

Do you follow up and make contact?

Are you sure you can offer a reciprocal arrangement to your contacts (win/win)?

Do you concentrate your efforts on those from whom you get a positive response?

Do you keep in regular, if brief, contact with a number of people?

Do you match-make among your web of contacts – fitting together those for whom the contact might be mutually advantageous?

Are you the person others come to because they know that you will know someone who can solve their problem?

If you are not that person, are you in contact with someone who is?

Would people describe you as a networker?

## chapter six

# Self-marketing

## … market yourself truthfully (but still show your best side)

When you think of 'marketing' or more pertinently, 'self-marketing', does it leave a sour taste in your mouth? It shouldn't, but perhaps it does. In the commercial and political worlds, unscrupulous marketers have given marketing a bad name, political spin being a prime example. And 'self-marketing' is seen as the territory of the over-confident brat. This poor reputation is undeserved in both cases.

## What is marketing really?

Effective marketing is not about lying, as some people believe, but exactly the opposite – it's about telling the truth. It requires deep knowledge of the product and the ability to disseminate that knowledge to those you wish to influence. It relies on recognising the value of your product and, by thoughtful presentation, exhibiting its worth. And, importantly, it is about looking for a niche into which your product will snugly fit.

In order to explain self-marketing, the above paragraph can be rewritten replacing 'product' with 'yourself' or 'your'.

Try it:

*Effective self-marketing is not about lying, as some people believe, but exactly the opposite – it's about telling the truth. It requires deep knowledge of yourself and the ability to disseminate that knowledge to those you wish to influence. It relies on recognising your value and, by thoughtful presentation, exhibiting your worth.*

*And, importantly, it is about looking for a niche into which you will snugly fit.*

This is the essence of marketing yourself:

- understanding your strengths (and weaknesses)
- communicating these to people who are influential in your life
- presenting yourself in a way that shows off your true value
- finding a niche where your value is maximised.

Selk-marketing is not to be confused with mere self-promotion or self-presentation – though these do form part of the self-marketing package. Effective self-marketing is not a surface gloss – it goes deep. If you want to stand out from the crowd yet still manage to fit in, you will need to self-market effectively.

Now, you might think that, of all the products we know, our understanding of ourselves would top the list. This is not so. Self-delusion can play some interesting tricks and self-reflection

'You can't fault him. He never misses a marketing opportunity'

can feel like navel gazing so is avoided. And sometimes, if we go deep down and admit it, we feel that it is just a mite risky putting ourselves into the potentially painful position of becoming more self-aware. It can be dangerous territory for the self-esteem so it needs to be approached with caution. Yet, if YOU don't know yourself well enough to maximise your potential, how on earth can THEY?

## Know yourself and value what you find

If you asked all the people who know you well to honestly describe your character, each would describe a different version of you. There would be similarities but the several descriptions would differ in important aspects. This difference is mediated by the filtering mechanisms working within their brains. Each of these people has a mental model of who you are and what you are like and will unconsciously filter out the signals which do no fit with this model. And the model they have of you is based on their level of knowledge and their relationship with you. So, your mother will see you differently from your best friend – phew, what a relief!

But how do we see ourselves? How have we built up our own model of ourselves? We all see things and people differently and this is the result of our own world view. We build up this world view over the early part of our lives and it is resistant to change. And we build our view of ourselves in the same way. It too is resistant to change – but that does not mean that it cannot be done. It just means that some things will take more time and effort than others. Depending on our innate differences and our early influences we turn out as either optimistic or pessimistic, extrovert or introvert, decisive or indecisive, confident or less confident etc etc. Our ragbag of personality traits combines to make us who we are. And thankfully there is no one, single, perfect personality; we are all different and all have value as a result. Just think what the world would be like if it were full of clones.

By the time we reach adulthood we are so used to the people that we have become that most of us never think in any serious way about ourselves and our effect on others. We never question whether we have turned out as we wanted to. We never really explore our strengths or our weaknesses. And we never get to know ourselves well enough to make the most of our individual attributes. This is because, by entering the process of getting to know ourselves better, we become vulnerable. We present ourselves with the possibility that we might get some nasty surprises. But rest assured! The likelihood of surprise is small because, deep down, most of us know ourselves pretty well and, fortunately, we also have those self-delusory mechanisms to fall back on.

## Signature strengths

In the past, the prevailing rationale for training and development was founded on a fallacy. It was thought that people should concentrate on improving their weaknesses and allow their strengths to take care of themselves. This was found to be rather less productive than expected and much time and energy was wasted by both teachers and learners. A much more effective regime for sustained improvement has come from the realm of positive psychology. This suggests that each of us has 'signature strengths'; a set of attributes which, because they come easily to us, give us the opportunity to excel. The evidence is that, by concentrating on further improving our strengths and finding a role or job which fits these strengths, we will increase both our efficiency and our effectiveness. And the bonus? We'll be happy and fulfilled in our work.

Unfortunately, this doesn't mean that we can safely ignore our weaknesses. These need some remedial action but the focus for most effort has moved from weaknesses to strengths because that's where the greatest pay-off lies.

# Some health warnings

However, before you even think of exploring your strengths and weaknesses, here are a few health warnings to think about.

**Health warning 1:** Introspection – Navel gazing can give you more than a crick in the neck.

Self-reflection is vital – it is our main mechanism for learning about ourselves. But it has some dangers. It can easily become an end in itself. You can become so bound up in your search for the truth about yourself that you forget that the real truth about yourself lies in your relationship with others. So don't spend too long looking inward – because outward is far more exciting. And don't take yourself too seriously!

**Health warning 2:** Self-esteem – Look after and cherish your self-esteem.

Our self-esteem is very precious. It cushions us against the hurt that the world can inflict on us. So, unless you are supremely confident or totally insensitive, your self-esteem is a fragile flower, and this flower is more delicate at some times than at others. If your self-confidence has taken a knock recently you may want to rebuild it before thinking further. And if you really don't like yourself, then the first stages for you will be focused on increasing your self-liking – and this may be accomplished simply by being nicer to other people. But whatever you do, try not to take *any* action which will damage your self-esteem.

**Health warning 3:** Perfectionism – Remember that nobody is perfect.

For some of us, it is easy to become too self-critical. So, concentrate on your strengths and don't try to be perfect. Remember – it's a likeable characteristic to have faults – our faults make everyone else feel so much better about their own! We admire perfection but we *like* people with flaws. It is probable that we all admired

71

Mother Teresa of Calcutta, but would we have wanted to go to the pub with her?

## Presenting yourself to the world

Your main strength might lie in your ability to empathise with others; it might be your spectacular brainpower or it could be that you are ace at tidying up the loose ends and finishing jobs that others have left undone. Whatever your strengths, if you hide them under a bushel or are in a job that doesn't suit them, you will not be maximising your potential. Having discovered your strengths and realised their value you need to do something with them.

Did you ever, as a child, walk on a high wall with a bed of nettles on one side and a gravel path the other? Falling off in either direction would have been painful. Self-marketing is like this but not as bad for the health! Both for self-marketing and for walking the wall, you need to gauge continually the path you are treading. We know what happens if we get it wrong with the wall. With self-presentation, if you go too far to one side and over-present, you will be seen as brash and over-confident (these are not likeable traits) and if you go too far the other way and under-present, you won't be seen at all!

At work, there are times when we are expected to market ourselves in a formal arena. Regular appraisal meetings provide the opportunity to show your strengths and your potential. Being asked to give a presentation to colleagues also provides the opening for you to show your worth. But as well as the formal set pieces, you should be self-marketing – in the best possible taste of course – continuously.

## Formal self-marketing

### Performance appraisal

If your workplace has an appraisal system whose purpose is your development (within the overall development of the organisation), your appraisal interview provides the opportunity for you to show your strengths and attributes and to admit to your weaknesses. It is also the ideal time for you to express your ambition for advancement and for suggesting the direction which you think it could take. Then a pertinent development plan can be put in place to increase your productivity. If you are in the unfortunate position of working in an organisation which sees appraisal solely as a means of distributing performance pay, then you will have to be much more circumspect about your failings.

## Making a presentation

The content of your presentation must be logical, relevant, well timed and with visual aids which are indeed aids to understanding and not simply crutches for you to lean on! There are many books which will assist with these aspects of presenting. In addition though, the most memorable presentations are always those which touch the emotions of the audience.

Before making a presentation, reread chapter 3 (communicating with head and heart). You could begin with a brief personal anecdote which is relevant to the subject and to the audience. This will bring your personality to the centre of the presentation and will provide that emotional pull that stories can generate. Your non-verbal signals can draw in your audience – especially those that show you to be a warm and open person.

And what of your visual aids? I've sat through hundreds, perhaps thousands, of presentations and the vast majority of these were instantly forgettable. There is one which stands out in my mind – although it must have been 15 years ago. The presenter used, for visual aids, a battered old teddy bear and an orange. Such was the impact that I can also remember the theme of the presentation and the name of the presenter. So, if you want to stand out, do something different. And, if you can leave them laughing or chatting enthusiastically, you'll have made your presentation memorable. They may not remember precisely what you said but they will certainly remember who said it!

## Finding the right niche

Our level of happiness depends to a large extent on whether we have found the right niche for ourselves. Here, I'm using 'happiness' in the Buddhist sense which relates closely to 'inner peace', or as the French say, 'being comfortable in your skin'. This is similar to the concept of psychological well-being – always a good thing to strive for! If you are engaged in work and play which fit with your underlying values, if you are with like-minded people working towards a valued goal and if your relationships with these people are open, warm and honest, you should thank your lucky stars – and the people around you. The conditions are in place for you to excel. There is, of course, more than one option. You can search to find the right niche or you can make it for yourself. You can look for a job which will suit both your intellectual ability and your personality or you can organise the job you have to play to your strengths and not to your weaknesses.

Self-marketing is easier for likeable people. They tend to understand themselves and be comfortable with the way they are. The key to self-marketing is knowing and liking yourself enough to be able to communicate your strengths to the world. And if you want to be likeable, it seems that communicating some of your weaknesses would also not be such a bad idea – depending, of course, on what those weaknesses are. If the weakness is brashness, over-confidence, pomposity or any of the dislikeable traits, it would be better to keep them to yourself and work on them privately!

# Thinking time

## Self-marketing

To think about: This is like showing your best side to the camera but not actually hiding your worst side. Formal self-marketing with your boss is best done through your appraisal system. Informal self-marketing is continuous – but remember to tread that fine line – to make sure you're visible but not seen as 'pushy'.

Do you understand your strengths and weaknesses?

Are you working to improve your 'signature strengths'?

Do you present these strengths to the world whilst working to eliminate your weaknesses?

Do you get the balance right between over- and under-presenting?

Have you found a niche where your true value can be maximised?

## chapter seven

# Leading

## ... attracting willing followers (and keeping them)

One of the growth industries of our time is writing about leadership. In any decent bookshop, the management shelves will be full of books about the who, the what and the how of leadership. And there are so many myths in circulation about this supposedly elusive quality. Let's debunk some of them!

## What leadership isn't

In the past there were just a few leaders and many, many followers. Throughout the 20th century, the captains of industry were a small and very select band. It was believed that they were a race apart; extraordinary people who were not like the rest of us. Even in the recent past, the ideal that was held up was that of the 'heroic leader'. This super-hero single-handedly rallied the troops (another military metaphor), and led them manfully (yes – they were *all* men) and charismatically (what is this charisma?) through the corporate jungle. It made for an exciting tale but, unfortunately for the fable makers, we all began to realise that this is not actually how leadership works. The heroic leader story was found to be fiction. And it was such a splendid story too!

The truth is that leadership is rather more complex – and yes, a little more boring – than that. Leaders aren't heroic figures who have some mystical powers that the rest of us can only dream of. They don't possess qualities which we, mere mortals, can aspire to but can't quite reach. And there is no fine line separating the

'Follow me. I know exactly where I'm going'

leaders from the led.  So, what happened to change our thinking?

What turned us all into leaders?  Were we all exhibiting some form of leadership no matter what our position in the hierarchy?  Or did someone coin the term 'distributed leadership' which led us to believe that we are all taking a leadership role?  No matter – the result is the same.  With distributed leadership, the expectation is that we will all be leaders. Tidy administration is not enough; excellent task management is not enough, carrying out our assigned duties perfectly is not enough.  With the current and future changes in the working environment, whatever your job, whatever your level in the workplace, you will also be expected to take a lead. This could be daunting but it needn't be; not if you understand the crux of leadership.

# What leadership is

It would be easy to become so enmeshed in the plethora of information and advice that the whole point of leadership is lost. So here it is in a nutshell:

*Leadership is a form of relationship. It is a relationship between leaders and their followers.*

And, in essence, that's *all* it is.

This may be counter-intuitive and hard to believe, but the power in this relationship lies absolutely in the hands of the followers. Astute leaders know this. Leaders can only lead when followers allow themselves to be led; and thus followers enter a tacit agreement with their leaders that they will follow. Followers often don't understand the extent of their power – which, for teachers in schools, is a thoroughly good thing! But in the adult world, the world of work, we are all required to lead, so where to start?

# What followers want

It's a logical impossibility to have a leader with no followers so central to leadership is the ability to attract and retain willing followers. When asked in a poll, the vast majority rated honesty as the most important attribute they would want in their leaders. And this takes us neatly back to Chapter 2 and all those attributes of likeable people.

For a few moments, think of yourself as a follower. Now think of your perfect manager at work – and it doesn't have to a real person! What type of leader would you follow?

- Would you want your leader to be a person in whom you can place absolute trust?
- Would you want to be sure they would respect confidences, and be open, straight and honest with you?
- And fulfil their commitments to you?
- Would you want them to trust you, even to the extent of

sharing their vulnerabilities with you?
- Do you want them to listen to you and to show care and consideration towards you?
- Would you wish them to show, by their response to you, that they like and value you as a person?
- And would you want them to be positive, optimistic and happy, spreading happiness wherever they go?

This sounds to me like someone I could easily follow. This list doesn't cover the full spectrum of leadership characteristics but forms a pretty powerful core. And these are all characteristics of likeable people. These are aspects of that elusive 'charisma' – that personal magnetism – which will attract people to your cause.

# Personal magnetism isn't enough

But there's more to leadership than a magnetic personality. Personal magnetism has its part to play in attracting and retaining followers but, to be an effective leader, more is needed. Being able to trust a leader's honesty is important but it is not the whole story. There is another aspect of trust to be considered. We must also be able to trust their judgement. Effective leaders know where they are going and communicate that knowledge to their followers.

Knowing where you're going requires an understanding of the environment you presently inhabit and a vision of the future environment you want to create. An understanding of the present comes with the decision to keep on learning. Vision and creation of the future are a little more complex. The basis of knowing where we are going is in knowing where we come from. Our vision of the future has its basis in our present value system. Those things we hold dear, those values which guide our actions; those are the things which form the basis of our decision-making and strategic thought. And values, vision and strategy need to be augmented by effective communication in order to grab the heads and hearts of those followers!

Effective leadership requires the leader to fit in by being likeable and stand out by having ideas, knowledge and strategic understanding and the ability to articulate all these. It's not easy – but being honest with your colleagues is a good place to start.

# Thinking time

## Leadership

To think about: Leadership is shot through with emotion and the great leaders in all spheres are those who are loved (yes, I did say loved) by their followers. The great military leaders fit into this category. If it's linear, and I'm not sure it is, excellent leaders would be loved, good leaders would be liked and mediocre ones tolerated. Which are you? And, as a leader, why would people trust you?

*1. Are you honest in your leadership style?*

Are you completely trustworthy?

Are you open, straight and honest with your followers?

Do you fulfil all your commitments to them?

Do you respect their confidences?

*2. Are you trusting?*

Do you share your vulnerabilities with them?

*3. Do you make your followers feel good about themselves?*

Do you listen to them?

Do you show care and consideration towards them?

Do you show that you value them both as a group and as individuals?

*4. Do you know where you are going?*

Can your followers trust your judgement?

Have you explored your personal values in order that they might underpin your decisions?

Do you take time to think about your vision of the future and the world you would want to create?

### 5. *Can you communicate your vision?*

Do you communicate in ways that engage both the heads and hearts of your followers?

Would people describe you as a good leader?

# chapter eight

# Learning

## ... how to stay half a step ahead

It is the nice, smart people who survive and prosper in a changing world. We've explored 'nice'. So, what about 'smart'? Smart people are the ones who manage to keep ahead of the game – and in a fast changing world that's not so easy. These people are continuous learners which means that they have open minds and are ready to grasp the opportunity to learn from any and every situation.

## How do we learn?

We have two main routes to learning. We learn from others – either in a formal teaching/training situation or informally through watching and listening to good practice. And of course, if we are adept learners, we ask intelligent questions and listen carefully to the answers.

But more importantly, we learn from our own experience. This 'trial and error' learning is more immediately useful because it lodges easily in our brains. We learn more readily from our own successes and failures than we do from seeing and hearing the experiences of others. We can learn a great deal from 'what works for us' but we learn even more from those attempts we make which can only be described as failures. So don't despair when things go wrong. Errors have huge value – if we make use of them. Remember the adage, 'The person who never made a mistake, never made anything!'

We all make mistakes but by reflecting on past experience we can ensure that we don't make the same mistake twice.

People's differing personalities will dictate the learning style which suits them best but there is one universal truth – learning comes easier if it is fun!

## Books, books, and more books

One important way to continue to learn from others' experience and to reflect on your own is to read voraciously. We are fortunate that we have the world at our keyboards and, as a consequence, many have foreseen the demise of books and bookshops. I think that reports of the death of the book have been greatly exaggerated. The sheer quantity of books available now makes choice almost impossible.

I find book shops magical places – libraries too. In a relatively small space they contain the accumulated wisdom, understanding, imagination, emotion, accomplishments, trials, tribulations and downright angst of thousands of extraordinary people. And these days, if we're lucky, there's a coffee shop too! My accountant can't believe how much I spend on books and the tax man hasn't queried it – yet. Books offer us the opportunity to experience life from the perspective of people we can never meet and to see the world through their eyes. The writers of these books might be the world's great thinkers or people like you and me but, if their words strike a chord, they will lodge in our hearts and minds and change us forever. If it isn't already your habit, do go and take a look – and see if you catch the magic.

Here is a selection of books that I have read and think worth recommending to you. These are topics that interest me – and that is the key to learning – you must find and read books which capture your interest and enjoyment. They might enhance your career path or change it completely or they might just make you a more interesting person. In our chaotic world we just have to be open to all possibilities! There are thousands, millions of books I haven't got round to yet. And if they are out of print I can trace them through the internet. So, why don't you go and haunt your local book shop or library – and see what treasure you can find.

## A Book that Changed my Life

**The Art of Happiness** by His Holiness the Dalai Lama and Howard C Cutler, Hodder and Stoughton 1998

If you think that we, in the West, have all the answers – or even that we understand the questions – then this book will teach you something. It is laid out as a series of conversations between the Dalai Lama and an American psychologist. The psychologist thoroughly annoyed me at first but by the end I quite liked him. The Dalai Lama is a legend; I can only think of Nelson Mandela who merits comparison.

## A Book about Changing Your Life

**Unstoppable People – how ordinary people achieve extraordinary things** by Adrian Gilpin, Random House 1998

This book tells a story. It begins with the author's discovery that he finds his business world uncomfortable, though he doesn't understand why, and then follows his journey through to fulfilment in both his business and private life. He discovered that his set of guiding values were at odds with the life he was living and set about moulding his life to reflect those values. If you take a similar path, I hope you won't have to begin at his starting point. His business venture collapsed and he lost just about everything – except the love and encouragement of his family. If you are dissatisfied and want to change I hope that your changes are of a rather more gentle variety!

## Attention

**The Attention Economy** by Thomas H Davenport and John C Beck, Harvard Business School Press 2002

This book was written primarily for organisations wishing to gain and manage both customer and employee attention. It could also be useful to anyone wanting to manage their own attention supply and to gain and hold the attention of others. Not for the faint-hearted.

## Bullying

**Bullying at work – how to confront and overcome it** by Andrea Adams, Virago 1992

Probably the first book on this subject and still the best that I know of. Workplace bullying is a serious issue as it can destroy people's lives. There are several organisations which assist the victims of workplace bullying including Trades Unions and Professional Associations. A good place to start is the Andrea Adams Trust in Hove, Sussex 01273 704 900 or www.andreaadamstrust.org This book can be obtained from the Trust.

## Chaos and Complexity

**The Art of Systems Thinking** by Joseph O'Connor and Ian McDermott, Thorsons 1997

We live in a world of interlinking systems which rely on feedback in order to remain stable and also in order to change. This practical book explains how you can leave behind linear thinking and make the most of the systems of which you are a part. And you'll even be able to astound your friends by knowing what cybernetics means.

**Turbulent Mirror** by John Briggs and F David Peat, Harper Perennial 1989

An illustrated guide to Chaos theory, it is a difficult read. I may have understood about a tenth of it – but then again, that might be an optimistic estimate. My self-image of an intelligent person won't allow me to admit quite how many times I lost the thread.

## Communication

**Peoplewatching** by Desmond Morris, Vintage 2002

**Manwatching** by Desmond Morris, Triad/Granada 1978

Updated and with two additional chapters, Peoplewatching has better content than its predecessor, Manwatching. Unfortunately, it also has inferior illustrations. Manwatching is out of print but both these books remain the first and most comprehensive exploration of non-verbal communication. You might be able to get a second hand copy of the original – it would be worth the effort.

**The Definitive Book of Body language** by Allan and Barbara Pease, Orion 2005

This is one of many self-help books written by Allan and Barbara Pease. This one is full of information to enable you to decipher the intricacies of facial expressions and bodily gestures. All their books are worth exploring.

**High Impact Presentations** by Lee Bowman, Bene Factum Publishing 2001

The content covers public speaking in a variety of contexts – the aim, to produce effective communication with any audience anywhere. It includes not only presentation skills but also influencing skills. Having retrieved it from my bookcase, I'm going to have to reread it.

**We, Me, Them & It, How to Write Powerfully for Business** by John Simmons, Cyan books 2006

This man is, quite obviously, conducting a love affair with words. And he understands their power to influence rather than merely to inform. He shows how there is competitive advantage for those who communicate well – and that includes individuals and the organisations they work for. The book is beautifully produced, the words flow effortlessly. It is a pleasure to read.

## The Future

**Evolve – Succeeding in the Digital Culture of Tomorrow** by Rosabeth Moss Kanter, Harvard Business School Press 2001

Rosabeth Moss Kanter is Professor of Business Administration at Harvard Business School. She asks a very big question; What difference will the Internet make to our lives? This book suggests that, in the e-world that we have entered, it will be networks of relationships which will release the energy and brainpower of e-business. Bliss – this book is not about technology but about people and the organisations for which they work.

**The Leader of the Future** edited by Frances Hesselbein, Marshal Goldsmith and Richard Beckhard, Jossey Bass Wiley 1997

This is one of the 'future' series from The Drucker Foundation (now called the Leader to Leader Institute), whose mission is 'to lead social sector organisations toward excellence in performance'. The eminent writers include Charles Handy, Peter Senge, Rosabeth Moss Kanter and the editors. All the contributors donated their time and effort and the book is dedicated to 'volunteers'. Whether you work in the public or private sectors or for a not-for-profit organisation, there are key messages here for you about the world we have entered.

**Connexity – How to Live in a Connected World** by Geoff Mulgan, Vintage 1998

This book questions how we can reconcile our desire for freedom and choice with the greater interdependence that comes with living in an increasingly interconnected world. It draws on ideas from psychology, philosphy, politics, economics, systems theory and computing and melds them into an accessible read. A clever man

– he was a founder director of Demos, an influential think-tank, and has moved on to work for the Young Foundation which is dedicated to finding new and better ways of meeting social needs.

**Relax, It's Only Uncertainty – lead the way when the way is changing** by Philip Hodgson and Randall P White, Pearson Education 2001

This is about being able to act without fear of failure; of being able to cope with ambiguity, of taking risks and reaching outside our comfort zone. It is well written, which is fortunate because it is a challenging read. Very well worth the effort though!

**Tilt - Irreverent lessons for leading innovation in the new economy** by Louis Patler, Capstone 2000

Isn't irreverence refreshing; and passion and engagement energising, and humour attractive – but only if it coincides with yours. For me, they are all here in a book which moves at breakneck speed from one original idea to another. Not a book for snails.

## Leadership

There are thousands of books on leadership and I've read dozens. Far too many are merely recycled ideas from the few creative thinkers about leadership. Here are books by two of those original and innovative authors:

**Old Dogs, New tricks** by Warren Bennis, Kogan Page 2000

Warren Bennis is Professor of Business Administration and Founding Chairman of the Leadership Institute at the University of Southern California. He also writes books that are very readable. He says that leaders need to engender trust, they need self-awareness and high self-esteem and to show compassion and empathy. They sound like pretty likeable people to me.

**Hesselbein on Leadership** by Frances Hesselbein, Jossey Bass Wiley 2002

Frances Hesselbein is Chairman and Founding President of the Drucker Foundation (now called the Leader to Leader Institute). As CEO of the Girl Scouts of the USA she led them from near irrelevance to become a thriving and vibrant institution with 4 million members. She describes leadership as 'a matter of how to be, not how to do it'. This book touched not a chord but a whole symphony in me. I would dearly love to meet this woman.

And two books by someone it would be a pleasure to work for:

**The Servant Leader**, Three Rivers Press 2004 and

**Love and Profit, the Art of Caring Leadership**, Avon Books NY 1991 both by James A Autry.

There is scant use of the words 'love' and 'caring' in business books. This second book bucks the trend. It is about leaders caring for their followers – but in some cases, it is tough love. In both, the author writes from 28 years experience of managing people and the lessons he has learnt along the way. He doesn't realise it but his approach is the one taken by outstanding military leaders – they are renowned for caring, above all, for the safety and well-being of their troops. I'll lay a bet that James Autry is a confident, competent and compassionate manager and leader. How rare is that?

**Business the Richard Branson way** by Des Dearlove   2002, Capstone

Supposedly this tells us the ten secrets of the world's greatest brand builder – but it is not the authorised version. Interesting in that it dissects the different style and substance of Branson's way of working. By no means is he a push-over – but what I like about Branson is that he does understand how to motivate people. He makes work fun!

## Marketing

**The Invisible Touch, the four Keys to Modern Marketing** by Harry Beckwith, Texere 2001

The book is aimed at people working in service industries and one of his four keys to successful marketing is the building of relationships. The book, and particularly this section, is relevant, not only to his target audience, but to all of us in everything we do. It forms a useful and readable self-marketing guide.

## Psychology

Psychology is the study of people. All human beings are psychologists to a greater or lesser extent because each of us has some level of understanding of ourselves and other people. By working to increase that understanding, we can gain insights which will enhance all aspects of our lives including our working lives.

**Beginning Psychology** by Malcolm Hardy and Steve Heyes, Oxford University Press 1999

This, or any other set book for a pre-university psychology course, will give an easy introduction and provide insights into memory, emotion, communication, learning, motivation, racial and gender stereotyping and other areas which will be of interest to those of you who want to understand what makes people tick.

**Vital Lies, Simple Truths, The Psychology of Self-deception** by Daniel Goleman, Bloomsbury 1998

First published in 1985, this book is, I think, Daniel Goleman's best work. It gives an in-depth analysis of how and why we all deceive ourselves. It outlines the part played by our very fallible memory in the construction of our present reality and the benefits and disadvantages of this universal self-deception. This one is a real eye-opener and very readable.

**The Creative Spirit** by Daniel Goleman, Paul Kaufman and Michael Ray, Plume 1993

This is Goleman's second best book. It was only published in the US and is unfortunately out of print. It has emotion as an underlying thread but in relation to creativity. And it declares that creativity is part of each of us. Unfortunately for our bosses we are all at our most creative in that twilight world between waking and sleeping – although I know some people at work who are always in this state! The section on vanquishing negativity at work is inspirational. Oh, that all of us could be lucky enough to work in a situation that is totally positive.

**Working with Emotional Intelligence** by Daniel Goleman, Bloomsbury 1999

There is little new in this world – just different ways of packaging the knowledge we have. Emotional intelligence is a clever way of repackaging previous knowledge about several positive aspects of human behaviour. Great – I have no problem with that – though some psychologists do. This book is more useful than Goleman's 'Emotional Intelligence' and gives some very helpful pointers to assist us in becoming emotionally competent at work. And there are huge overlaps between likeability and EI.

**Authentic Happiness** by Martin E P Seligman, Nicholas Brealey 2003

Seligman could be described as the founder of the 'positive psychology' movement which re-orientates psychology towards a better understanding of psychological well-being. His definition of happiness goes deeper than just enjoyment. As a result of his research, he has found three components of happiness: pleasure (the smiley-face bit), engagement (the depth of involvement with one's family, work, romance and hobbies) and meaning (using personal strengths to serve some larger end). Of those three roads to a happy, satisfied life, he believes pleasure is the least consequential.

That's my list of 'all time greats' – the ones I keep going back to. Your list will be different but whatever is in it – Happy reading!

# Thinking time

## Learning

To think about: the key to learning is being open to experience and willing to change.

### 1. Do you learn from others?

Do you take all available opportunities to engage in appropriate training and development events?

After the event, do you write down one key point you want to work on?

Do you take all available opportunities to learn from your colleagues?

Do you always have a book on the go?

### 2. Do you learn from yourself?

Do you take the time to analyse your past successes to see what went right – and what you could improve on?

And more importantly, do you analyse your failures to make sure you don't repeat mistakes?

## chapter nine

# What next?

## ... what to do about it

## The story so far

The world is changing faster now than ever before and in order to ensure our continued success in this new world, we must change too. We know that the world of the future will be different from the world of the past but we (individually) don't know what it will be like because we (collectively) haven't invented it yet. And that is the one big message of this book – to a large extent, we invent our own future; we create our own world. By our individual choices and actions we create our immediate environment and change the future in small ways. By our collective action we set the direction of the huge changes that will create our brave new world. But that's for another book! Let's just concentrate on your immediate surroundings; your world of work. In your own small world, not only can you adapt to meet new circumstances, but by early adaptation, you can be the one who creates the future. But whether you want to create the future or be ready to meet it or if you simply want to make the present a happier place to be – you can do it. And if you think you're too small to make a difference, you have, quite obviously, never been in bed with a mosquito!

The future world of work will require us to be ever ready to change job, career, direction. In order to prepare for the future, and also to improve the present, we can make changes in the way we think and behave. Changing behaviour is the easy part; changing underlying attitudes and values – that comes harder. If you want to make the most of the opportunities on offer and be one of those nice, smart people who can simultaneously fit in and stand out, you might need to make a few changes.

# Making choices

At this point you have a choice. You can decide that:

(a) This book has been very / mildly / not at all interesting and you're happy as you are and don't want to disturb your equilibrium.

(b) It has raised some questions that you want to reflect on and this might or might not include asking other people for their views.

(c) You think you might want to make some changes but you don't know what.

(d) You know you want to make some changes and you know precisely what you want to do.

For the (a) people – thanks, I do hope you've gained something. I wish you the very best for the future.

For the (b), (c), (d) people, read on:

# Making changes

We are forever making changes in our lives which go wrong. We decide we want to change job, go for promotion, lose weight, stop smoking or find the perfect partner and it doesn't work out as planned. There are two reasons for this, (1) we don't understand how successful change works and (2) we are so impatient for results that we take on too much too quickly.

# Lasting change – elusive but possible

In a nutshell, change is like a journey. To get from A to B:

1. We want to go there.

2. We look at a map to find out where B is.

3.  We plan the route and the means of travel.

4.  We start out from A

And eventually we get to B.

If we miss out one of these steps, B will be yet another place that we've never managed to visit. So, if just one element is missing, we are very unlikely to get what we want. We may be lucky and stumble on a solution but it's by no means guaranteed. If we leave out two steps - no chance!

And talking of steps - lasting change comes in very small steps. In between these small steps are pauses for breath in order for that change to bed down. If you try to rush the process, it will fall apart. Anyone who has successfully painted a room knows that you have to wait for one coat of paint to dry before applying another. All successful change efforts follow this same principle – and we all know what people say about watching paint dry, but it is a necessary part of the process.

'Next stage, we get to wear our underpants INside'

All intentional changes, from the smallest personal changes right up to the huge change programmes in big business, follow the same process whose vital constituent parts are precisely the same.

Think of successful change as a chain reaction. All the components must be present; just one missing link will cause the chain to fall apart.

## The four step change programme

These essentials for getting from A to B can be converted into a programme for change. Here is a Four-Step Change programme. The vital links are:

1. We want to go there. We are dissatisfied with the status quo.

In order to 'want to go there' we need to be dissatisfied with the current state of affairs and want to make some changes. And the more uncomfortable we are with our current state, the more likely we are to start the process. If we are happy with the way we are, we will not change – no matter how much other people nag us! And why should we? Change always brings discomfort, especially at the start, so we all need an impetus to get us going.

Missing out step 1; If we don't take that initial decision to make a change, nothing will happen.

So: no dissatisfaction = no change

2. We look at a map to find out where B is. We have a vision of where we want to get to.

A sense of the direction in which we'll travel shows us how things can improve; what the possible outcomes are, what we can gain. It gives an idea of what things will be like when we reach our goal – but we need to be realistic about this. Most change programmes don't bring earth-shattering results. However, it is important to know how much better things can be because all change involves some pain (or at least, discomfort) particularly in the early stages.

So, it is reasonable to ask 'why pain if no gain?'

Missing out step 2; if we haven't worked out where we want to go, we have little chance of reaching our destination. We'll set in place plans but will they have the desired result? Probably not – because we're not even sure what the desired result is!

So no vision/direction = unfocussed change

3. We plan the route and the means of travel. We produce some sort of plan for improvement.

A 'plan for improvement' does not have to be a detailed step by step guide but it does have to include understanding of what to do next in order to move in the right direction. Some people will want to have a complete step by step guide before setting out, others will prefer to be more flexible and decide the next steps as they go. Both strategies can work as long as we keep our goal in mind and plan the way to it.

Missing out step 3; here, we know we want to change, we have some idea where we want to get to so we move straight on to step 4. But we haven't given any thought to the speed, direction or type of change – we just go for it – the scattergun approach. The process might work it is not optimal or anywhere near.

So no plan for improvement = arbitrary change

4. We start out. We take our first steps.

And 'first steps' means actually doing something. We've thought it through (well, some of it). Now we have to put it into action. And once we've taken the first steps, the second, third and fourth become much easier.

Missing out step 4; all the thinking has been done but there is no action.

So no first steps = stalled change

The positions of dissatisfaction and vision can be reversed. We might be dissatisfied and be looking for a solution or we might see the possibility of a change for the better and that makes us dissatisfied with what we have. But whatever their relationship in time, it is imperative that all the links are in place because if just one element is missing, things can go seriously awry.

## Some more health warnings

Before starting out to make changes, it is worth considering these Health Warnings. (Health Warnings 1,2 and 3 are repeated. They appeared first in Ch 6)

**Health warning 1:** Introspection – Navel gazing can give you more than a crick in the neck.

Self-reflection is vital – it is our main mechanism for learning about ourselves. But it has some dangers. It can easily become an end in itself. We can become so bound up in our search for the truth about ourselves that we forget that the real truth about ourselves lies in our relationship with others. So don't spend too long looking inward – because outward is far more exciting. And don't take yourself too seriously!

**Health warning 2:** Self-esteem – Look after and cherish your self-esteem.

Our self-esteem is very precious. It cushions us against the hurt that the world can inflict on us. Unless we are supremely confident or totally insensitive, our self-esteem is a fragile flower, and this flower is more delicate at some times than at others. If your self confidence has taken a knock recently you may want to rebuild it before thinking further. And if you really don't like yourself, then the first stages for you will be focused on increasing your self-liking - and this may be accomplished simply by being nicer to other people. But whatever you do, try not to take *any* action which will damage your self-esteem.

**Health warning 3:** Perfectionism – Remember that nobody is perfect.

For some of us, it is easy to become too self-critical. So, concentrate on your strengths and don't try to be perfect. Remember – it's a likeable characteristic to have faults – our faults make everyone else feel so much better about their own! We admire perfection but we *like* people with flaws.

**Health warning 4:** Emotional control – We don't have to scream and shout.

We have little control over the emotions we experience but we do have a great deal of control over our actions. However deeply you feel emotion, it is your choice whether and how you express those feelings through your behaviour. You don't have to be prey to your emotions. Your rational self can exercise choice about your response. Intemperate behaviour which causes distress or even unease in others is destructive to the perpetrator, the recipient and their relationship. It is an indulgence we should not allow ourselves.

**Health warning 5:** Ambiguous signals – You can find yourself in deep water just by being friendly.

The liking/loving/sexual attraction signals that we give and receive are very similar. Positive emotion is positive emotion and we can't always foretell people's reaction. Be aware that your signals might be misinterpreted so, go gently. When you engage people's emotions they will reciprocate and, almost always, this will be pleasant for you both. But emotions can be sleeping tigers. On rare occasions you may meet someone whose need for emotional engagement is so strong that you begin to feel overwhelmed. Do not feel guilty if you find that you need to retreat. Their needs and problems are not your responsibility. Your only responsibility is to try to limit any damage – but it will not always be possible to eliminate it completely.

**Health warning 6:** Sincerity – You can't fake sincerity.

Not for long anyway. Eventually you will be rumbled. Becoming more attractive to people involves valuing them for what they are – not for what you think they can do for you. If you want to increase the health of your relationships, think win/win. If you try to fool people and they find out – and this will happen eventually – their liking of you will flip over into dislike. Is it worth the risk?

# Moving forward

Increasing your personal magnetism; drawing people to you – well, the trick is to enhance both the number and strength of your likeable traits and eliminate any dislikeable ones – to value other people and not to damage them. But HOW DO WE KNOW if we behave in a way that makes us likeable? We need to ask ourselves some difficult questions and give some honest answers. With Health Warning 1 (introspection) in mind, this should not be prolonged and angst ridden. And what do others think of us? The best way to find out is to ask them. Bearing in mind Health Warning 2 (self-esteem), be careful who you choose to ask. You need to choose people who will be honest but not brutally honest. And you can prepare them for the task by setting the parameters. Tell them about preserving your self-esteem whilst giving you pointers for improvement. Tell them about Health Warning 3 – that you think you can only manage one or two areas at a time so could they think carefully about which are the most important. Then give them all or part of the the section headed 'Questions, questions'. You could ask just one friend or divide the questionnaire between several.

# Nice

In addition to the traits associated with being likeable, your communicative style is the key to improving your relationships and increasing your sphere of influence. And this all impacts on your ability to lead, self-market and network. So the three key areas to concentrate on, in the first instance, are likeable and dislikeable traits and communication – the others will follow from these.

## And smart

Those who are continuous learners are already open to changes which will increase their attractiveness. But it's also important to be open to new skills and ideas and ways of thinking.

## Build your own bridges

I've given you a box full of building bricks. Now it's for you to build your own bridges to your specification and satisfaction. They will all be different – there is no template. You will take only those bricks that you need and will use them to build and strengthen your relationships. But remember this – your bridges will be more robust if you enjoy building them. So, in the midst of all your building materials, remember that there is one very important component. It should be fun!

# And finally

## ... I have a dream

People are precious. They have intrinsic value which has its basis in our shared humanity. They are equal partners with us in our attempts to mould our world. We should look after them – they deserve it, but we should also look after ourselves because we deserve it too.

I believe that we are all agents of our own destiny who invent the future for ourselves so here's my final question for you:

What if it were possible for us to create a world where everyone, in every relationship and encounter, were to strive for a win/win outcome?

What a happy and successful world that would be. Heaven on earth – yep, can't be bad.

# Acknowledgements

## ... with a little help from my friends

This is the book equivalent of the Oscar acceptance speech. They're allowed exactly one minute so, short and to the point is best. I don't have a Key Grip, Best Boy or Personal Hair Stylist, but I now realise that books, like films, can have a cast of thousands. This is my cast list. I thank them all:

Those who allowed me free access to their thought processes through honest and considered interview – John Adams, Stephen Adamson, Brian Gilbert, Anita Metcalfe, Diana Penton, Amy Phillips, Ralph Tabberer, Judith Wilson, Mike Wilson.

Diana Penton, Sian Phillips, Mike Wilson – who allowed me to publish their private emails.

Amy Phillips – the person who made sure I got the physics right.

Blake Pheasey – who carefully produced cartoons to my sometimes inexact specifications.

Genevieve Hayman, Helen Bevis and Amy Phillips – who patiently read the drafts and answered my damn fool questions.

And the many people who form my email networks, with special thanks to Jane Woodnutt, but also to all those – and there are many of them – who waded in to help when I needed it.

At Oscar ceremonies they have the award for Best Supporting Actor. Mine is called Glyn. He puts up with me manfully and gives me the confidence and stability which allow me to step bravely into the world.

# Questions, Questions
## ... with a little help from your friends

Your friend has been reading a book about personal magnetism and how this can help them in their career. You can help by answering these questions.

All the questions require a yes / no answer. But you are not looking for perfection. Be honest but also sensitive to your friend's feelings and write additional comments if you think this will be helpful. If you really can't answer any question, just put 'don't know'.

This is not a test and there's no good or bad score. The purpose of all these questions is to help your friend to think about how they can increase their chances of getting on – both in their career and with other people; to manage the two opposites – fitting in, yet standing out from the crowd.

To get round the problem of gender – he and she, him and her, his and hers – I have used the plural them and their. This is purely for ease even though it is a bit clumsy.

## Likeable traits are all related to valuing people

### 1. Is your friend trustworthy?

To think about: Trustworthiness is really important because it and its opposite feature highly in people's likes and dislikes. People who are discrete, honest and reliable are good friends and if they want to have good friends, they will need to be a good friend. We spent most of our waking hours at work so making and keeping good friends at work will also make life much more productive and enjoyable.

Do they always keep secrets?

When people tell them some intimate or sensitive information, can these people be sure that it will go no further?

Do they always tell the truth but try to do so in a way that ensures that damage to others is minimised?

Do they always try hard to fulfil their commitments to others?

If they are unable to keep their promise, do they tell people in good time?

Would people describe them as a good friend to have?

Would people describe them as trustworthy?

### 2. Is your friend trusting?

To think about: On the whole, people live up to our expectations of them but, on occasion, they let us down. So, there will be breaches of trust. That's life. It takes both self-confidence and confidence in others for your friend to trust others enough to show their weaknesses and vulnerabilities. But if they do, the emotional impact on the recipient of their trust will be substantial. If that person is worthy of their trust it will build a bond that will be difficult to break.

Do they trust people until they have reason to do otherwise?

Do they share both their strengths and their weaknesses with the people they trust?

Do they share their real vulnerabilities with the people they trust implicitly?

Would people describe them as trusting?

### 3. Do they show that they like people?

To think about: We all get so confused by ambiguous signals – and we all give out ambiguous signals. Being more direct in their approach but also more thoughtful about the impact – they don't want to frighten the horses – could make life so much more simple.

Do they tell people – in words of one syllable – that they like them?

When they are with people they like, do they give them their full attention?

Do they go out of their way to help them?

Do they joke with them and tease them?

Do they show that they are relaxed and comfortable in their company?

Do they smile at them – with both their lips and their eyes?

Do they touch them?

### *4. Do they make people feel good about themselves?*

To think about: It is so easy to get caught up in the millions of tasks that we all have to undertake and to forget the little things which can bring joy to others. Just remembering to thank people or asking about their new car, their child's exams or their holiday in Slovenia (remembering where they went gets them bonus points!) will make people feel that they are valued. Of course, if they're not really interested - then they shouldn't bother asking.

Tough one this! Do they show care and consideration towards both the people they like and those they don't like?

Do they really listen to people?

Are they sensitive to others' moods and change their behaviour to suit?

Do they resist the urge to pass judgement on others?

Do they forgive other people for their flaws?

Are they positive, optimistic and happy – and do they spread happiness wherever they go?

Are they fun to be with?

Would you describe them as kind and considerate?

## Dislikeable traits are all related to causing damage to other people

It is hard to suggest that any of these might apply – but remember, nobody's perfect. Just look through to see if any of the questions raise doubts in your mind. But do be gentle with them!

### 1. Is your friend selfish and manipulative?

To think about: This is an area it is difficult to address but, if they have always been encouraged to be competitive, especially in their childhood, it is easy to fall into the trap of habitually putting themselves first. They may think that win/lose is the only option available to them. Becoming more co-operative and less competitive will not be easy, but the benefits of moving from win/lose to win/win are considerable – and well worth the effort.

Do they cause or encourage conflict between people?

Do they use other people for their own advantage?

Do they look for weaknesses in others and use these against them?

Do they use their strengths as levers to gain advantage over others?

Do people become their victims?

Do they look for a win/lose outcome?

Would you describe them as competitive?

Would you describe them as selfish?

Would you describe them as manipulative?

### 2. Is your friend a bully?

To think about: We have all heard of out-and-out bullies who make life unbearable for others. With malicious purpose, they set out to destroy the confidence of their victims. But what of the rest of us? We can, all of us, unwittingly be the perpetrators of bullying behaviour. Your friend may think that sarcastic comments or put-downs are funny. To the recipient, they are certainly not funny, and to the audience, they are often embarrassing. Bolstering their confidence by belittling others will rebound on them and will win them no friends, just enemies. Bolstering the confidence of others by kind and helpful comments will have the opposite effect – and the rebound will be positive for their confidence too.

Do they administer public put-downs?

Do they use sarcasm?

In giving negative feedback, do they criticise the person not their action?

Do they gossip about people in an unkind way behind their backs?

Do they encourage malicious rumours and gossip?

Do they set unreasonable goals with the expectation that they will not be reached?

### 3. Is your friend untrustworthy?

To think about: It can take just one instance of indiscreet, dishonest or unreliable behaviour for trust to be lost completely – especially if the recipient is already feeling vulnerable. Once trust is lost, it is very difficult to regain. Prevention is so much better than cure.

Have they ever betrayed a confidence?

Have they ever betrayed someone's trust?

Have they ever told a lie to get themselves out of trouble?

Have they ever told a lie which hurt or damaged someone else?

Have they ever withheld information so that the person who needed that information was disadvantaged?

Have they ever let someone down because they could not fulfil a commitment they had entered into?

Would you describe them as indiscreet?

Would you describe them as dishonest?

Would you describe them as unreliable?

### 4. Are they overly self-centred?

To think about: Again, not easy to own up to, but sometimes we just take life too seriously. These traits can all be lessened by taking a more relaxed attitude to life in general. Accepting that everyone has faults makes it easier to be kind to them. The next step is to forgive both themselves and others because we all have shortcomings.

Do they take themselves too seriously?

Do they either ignore or refuse to listen to other people's points of view?

Do they undervalue the views of others?

Do they judge other people and find them wanting?

Would you describe them as self-important and pompous?

Would you describe them as prejudiced and judgmental?

Would you describe them as self-centred?

### 5. Are they mean?

To think about: It may just be thoughtlessness but ungenerous behaviour does rankle with people.

Are they overly concerned with money and possessions?

Do they get bound up in small and unimportant details causing others to become annoyed?

Are they always the last person to buy their round in the pub?

Would you describe them as small-minded?

Would you describe them as avaricious or mean?

*6. Are they insensitive?*

Do they upset people without noticing?

Are they oblivious to the effect they have on other people?

Are they inept at picking up other people's verbal and non-verbal cues?

Are they unable to put themselves in other people's shoes?

Would you describe them as insensitive?

## Communicating with head and heart

*1. Does your friend communicate clearly?*

To think about: Lack of clarity leads to so many miscommunications which, in turn, lead to misunderstanding and the potential souring of relations. With just a little thought, the clarity of their communications can improve dramatically.

In all their communications, either spoken or written, do they ensure that there is complete understanding?

Do they summarise at intervals and ask for feedback to ensure clarity and mutual understanding?

Are they aware of the non-verbal signals they transmit?

Do their verbal and non-verbal signals give out the same message?

Would you describe both their written and spoken communications as clear and unambiguous?

### 2. Do they communicate with sensitivity?

To think about: We cannot know for certain how people will respond to our communications. However, some consideration of the possible impact will help to produce the effect they desire rather than some random effect over which they have no control.

Do they ensure that they communicate with the right people at the right time so that people feel included and informed?

Do they consider the impact on the recipient of all their written and verbal utterances?

Do they choose their words carefully so as to ensure that they do not offend?

Would you describe their communications as sensitive?

### 3. Do their communications engage people's emotions?

To think about: If they want to influence people, then they must make them laugh, cry, smile, punch the air – or give any signal which tells them that they are emotionally engaged. It also helps if what they say makes sense!

Do their communications tell a story?

Do they choose their words carefully so as to elicit positive emotions?

Do they use analogy and metaphor to increase the richness of their communication?

Do they expose some of themselves and their emotions in their communications?

Do they use non-verbal signals, especially eye-contact and touch to increase the emotional impact of their communication?

Would you say that people enjoyed receiving their communications?

### 4. Are their communications reciprocal?

To think about: We tend to concentrate on our side of the dialogue – the speaking and writing. But it *is* a dialogue – and listening and reading are probably of greater importance to us, because it is through these that we learn.

In their communications do they always ensure that there the opportunity for dialogue?

Do they allow other people to influence them?

Do they actively listen and read – and this means giving all of their attention when others communicate with them?

Do they always respond when others contact them, even if only to say 'thanks but no thanks'?

Do they always respond in an encouraging and constructive way to the communications of others?

Would you describe them as a good communicator?

## Networking

To think about: The very effective networkers spend much of their time networking. But they don't see it as a separate task – it is an integral part of all that they do. There is a networking strand in all their encounters and they constantly pick up and store information for later use – and they are always looking for win/win.

Do they make a habit of getting contact details from people they meet?

Do they make sure that they remember pertinent facts about them?

Do they follow up and make contact?

Do they ensure that they can offer a reciprocal arrangement to their contacts (win/win)?

Do they concentrate their efforts on those from whom they get a positive response?

Do they keep in regular, if brief, contact with a number of people?

Do they matchmake among their web of contacts – fitting together those for whom the contact might be mutually advantageous?

Is your friend the person that others come to because they know that they will know someone who can solve the problem?

If they are not that person, are they in contact with someone who is?

Would people describe them as a networker?

## Self-marketing

To think about: This is like showing their best side to the camera but not actually hiding their worst side. Formal self-marketing with their boss is best done through their appraisal system. Informal self-marketing is continuous – but remember – they shouldn't be seen as 'pushy'.

Do they understand their strengths and weaknesses?

Are they working to improve their strengths?

Do they present their strengths to the world whilst working to eliminate their weaknesses?

Do they get the balance right between over-presenting and under-presenting?

Have they found a niche where their true value can be maximised?

## Leadership

To think about: Leadership is shot through with emotion and the great leaders in all spheres are those who are loved (yes, I did say loved) by their followers. The great military leaders fit into this category. If it's linear, and I'm not sure it is, excellent leaders would be loved, good leaders would be liked and mediocre ones tolerated. Which are they? And, as a leader, why would people trust them?

*1. Are they honest in their leadership style?*

Are they completely trustworthy?

Are they open, straight and honest with their followers?

Do they fulfil all their commitments to them?

Do they respect their confidences?

*2. Are they trusting?*

Do they share their vulnerabilities with them?

*3. Do they make their followers feel good about themselves?*

Do they listen to them?

Do they show care and consideration towards them?

Do they show that they value them both as a group and as individuals?

*4. Do they know where they are going?*

Can their followers trust their judgement?

Have they explored their personal values in order that these might underpin their decisions?

Do they take time to think about their vision of the future and the world they would want to create?

*5. Can they communicate their vision?*

Do they communicate in ways that engage both the heads and hearts of their followers?

Would people describe them as a good leader?

## Learning

To think about: the key to learning is being open to experience and willing to change.

### *1. Do they learn from others?*

Do they take all available opportunities to engage in appropriate training and development events?

After the event, do they write down one key point they want to work on?

Do they take all available opportunities to learn from their colleagues?

Do they always have a book on the go?

### *2. Do they learn from themselves?*

Do they take the time to analyse their past successes to see what went right – and what they could improve on?

And more importantly, do they analyse their failures to make sure they don't repeat mistakes?

# About the author

After a first career as a school teacher, Jane Phillips undertook two further periods of formal education and gained a BA in psychology from the Open University and an MSc in Occupational Psychology from the University of Hertfordshire. She worked for 15 years as a Business Psychologist and now writes full time. Her published work includes numerous articles and two books. The books are diverse; the first describes staff selection techniques and the second, written in collaboration with a French chef, is a dual language recipe book about a French hotel and its superb home-made jam. She is married with two grown-up children and lives in Cambridge.

## By the author

### L'Armoire à confitures - Jam in the cupboard

If you love France or love good food then "Jam in the cupboard" is the book for you. It has recipes, stories and sumptuous photographs which together celebrate the 65 varieties of jam made and served at the Hotel Diderot in Chinon.

Written in both French and English jointly by Jane and Glyn Phillips and Laurent Dutheil, the jam expert at the hotel Diderot, this book reveals some of the secrets and joys of jam making.

More details at www.jaminthecupboard.com

121

## Recruitment and Selection: A practical guide for school governors and headteachers

One of the most important tasks performed by any governing body is the appointment of a new headteacher or deputy. It requires skills and knowledge - many of which apply also to making any staff appointment - but with the correct guidance these can be quickly acquired for the task.

This book provides exactly the guidance needed for all those involved with making appointments. It explains the principles behind all staff appointments, with particular reference to those of the headteacher or deputy. It lays out step by step the procedures that have to be followed, and, drawing on the work of leading management experts, shows how to use the time and tools available to best assess exactly how the candidates meet your requirements.

The book also includes various documents that can be adapted for your own use, including the job description, person specification, advert, applicants' pack, request for references, and forms for assessing candidates in the interview and their presentation. These can also be bought with the book on CD ROM so they can be downloaded and adapted.

More information at www.adamsonbooks.com